Ask Erica

ERICA WILSON

D1502011

**NEWSPAPERBOOKS
AND CHARLES SCRIBNER'S SONS**

NEW YORK

BOOKS BY ERICA WILSON

Needleplay
The Craft of Black Work and White Work
Erica Wilson's Embroidery Book
The Craft of Crewel Embroidery
Fun with Crewel Embroidery
Crewel Embroidery

Copyright © 1977 Erica Wilson

Copyright © 1976, 1977 Chicago Tribune-New York News Syndicate, Inc.

Erica Wilson's newspaper column *Needleplay* provides the basis for some of the answers in this book.

Library of Congress Cataloging in Publication Data
Wilson, Erica.
    Ask Erica.

    Includes index.
    1. Needlework–Miscellanea. 2. Embroidery–Miscellanea.
I. Title.
TT751.W53 746.4'4 77-11617
ISBN 0-684-15296-7
ISBN 0-684-15295-9 pbk.

1 3 5 7 9 11 13 15 17 19 M/C 20 18 16 14 12 10 8 6 4 2

1 3 5 7 9 11 13 15 17 19 M/P 20 18 16 14 12 10 8 6 4 2

Printed in the United States of America

INTRODUCTION

What a delightful experience it has been really getting to know so many of the people who, as I do, find such pleasure in that most satisfying of all the arts, needlework. In the last decade or so, I think I've traveled to just about every state in the Union, giving talks and even lectures demonstrating the many different kinds of arts and techniques included in that one word, needlework. (I like to boast about my coast-to-coast knowledge of America because, as you may know, I'm actually British by birth and grew up in Devonshire.) And then, when it seemed that I had "covered the territory" from Maine to California, my husband thought of a charming variation: put Erica out to sea! So off we went, a group of eager needlewomen (and men) on a cruise to Nassau and Bermuda, spending mornings learning more about the craft and afternoons relaxing under a beautiful Atlantic blue sky!

But if I've met literally thousands of you, many more thousands of you have come to know me through my books, through the syndicated newspaper column *Needleplay* and my two television series called "Erica." I was a bit hesitant at first about appearing on television — what husband would miss a ball game to allow his wife to watch *her* favorite sport? And who would have time for needlework in the middle of a Wednesday afternoon, or Thursday evening or whenever? Then the mail began to pour in and I was reassured that I wasn't an unwelcomed guest in your living room. But what was more important to me than this personal satisfaction was the proof that there really is an audience eager to spend the time learning how to create so many beautiful things.

Well, it has been a marvelous two-way affair — and that's how this book came to be. The scores and scores of questions that I've gathered together here were selected out of thousands that have been asked of me on my tours, after lectures and demonstrations, and through the mail. It wasn't easy to sort through those mail sacks, I assure you! Nor was it easy to decide just what questions and problems were the ones most people had. Persistence and patience, as I always tell my beginning needleworkers! I began to see that certain problems always arose — What stitch should I use? How do I transfer my design to the canvas? How do I clean and block my finished project? And even seasoned nonbeginners sometimes stop and realize they've never threaded a needle properly! Naturally, I had to put answers to all these questions in my book, and, of course, I had to decide what would be the best way to arrange the answers so you could go immediately to the answer. I don't know about you, but I find some reference books like the proverbial backscratcher that's just a hair too short to reach where it itches. By arranging all the answers alphabetically, from A to Z, I hope I save you some unnecessary "scratching around" for the answer to your question.

Even though I was fortunate in having excellent needlework teachers, and have had many years of experience, I sometimes feel I'm only one jump ahead of my students—and that's why there are so many questions in this book about the latest "news" in needlework. Word does get around, and the questions do eventually get to me: What about this plastic canvas? Can I really have a photograph painted on my canvas? My grandmother did smocking, why can't I? Is gold work just for museums? Did I hear you say *crewelpoint?*

I think as you read this book, you'll come to agree with me that "needlework" is one of those umbrella words, with so many things crowded under it that it does take at least the entire alphabet to spell it all out. If you're a beginner, I hope *Ask Erica* will become your "first reader." If you're an expert, I hope you'll find some new slant, a new angle of vision, to increase your joy in your work. People tell me we are living in an age of fast, cheap and shoddy things. I don't believe it for one minute! The needleworkers I've come to know are dedicated, inventive craftsmen and—the honor is yours—artists.

Erica Wilson

Algerian Eyelet Stitch

What can I do to get my Algerian eyelet stitches to look smooth and clearcut?

The secret of the Algerian eyelet stitch is to keep a clear, open hole in the center as you work the satin stitches evenly side by side around it, never letting the stitches overlap one another. Start by gently opening a hole in the canvas by inserting the points of a closed pair of scissors. (Be careful not to tear the canvas!) As you stitch, always go down in the center, rotating the needle in the hole to force it open. Pull firmly as you take each stitch smoothly side by side, to hold the hole open. The diagram shows the eyelet being worked over 4 threads, but you can work over as many as you like, to about 6 or 8 threads. More than this may fill up the center hole, into which all the stitches have to be worked.

Appliqué

Help! The very first shape of my appliqué wall panel puckered when I sewed it down. How can I make my cutouts lie flat when I assemble them?

Rush to the notion store for that wonderful Pellon you can iron to the back of your fabric. Cut out the shape close around the outline— the iron-on gauzy muslin holds the fabric firm and it's like cutting out paper. Now stretch the base fabric tightly in a frame and baste the appliqué pieces down. Stretch the fabric taut and sew the shapes down, using small invisible stitches (at right angles to the edges), using one strand of sewing cotton. Bring the needle up outside the shape, then down through the appliqué, so that the piece will lie flat and not be poked out of place as you stitch.

My great-grandmother is asking me to do needlework for her! I must say I'm flattered, but I'm also bewildered by what she would like—something she calls "Sabrina work." I'd like to do the appliqué for her, but I can't find any reference to this kind of needlework. Can you help me?

Isn't it nice to be able to keep an old art alive, especially one as lovely as Sabrina work? Sabrina is made by cutting pieces of velvets, silks or cotton into leaves, flower petals or butterflies, natural or stylized. The pieces are gathered or folded at the base of each petal and then appliquéd to a background material so that they stand out in relief. The result, as your great-grandmother no doubt recalls, is very rich and elegant. That is probably the reason that the art was so popular during the plush, gilt-and-velvet days that characterized the nineteenth century.

I've just assembled, rather neatly, if I do say so, an appliqué wall hanging. But on closer inspection, I think it needs something much more interesting-looking than the simple invisible stitches with which I held each piece down. What can I do now?

Why not make the method of attaching your appliqué pieces an integral part of the overall design? For example, if your design allows for it, you could sew down the appliqué pieces with a bold blanket stitch or a herringbone in a contrasting color. There are many decorative stitches that can be used to outline the edge of your appliqué pieces. A chain or stem stitch might be the perfect finishing touch. Of course, a frankly decorative stitch should have been part of your original design concept—a blanket stitch edging can change the whole effect. But sometimes one can only tell that a darker accent in chain or stem stitch is needed when the work is done.

Appliqué, Reverse

On a recent trip to Panama, I saw some very colorful skirts and blouses made by the San Blas Indians. Can you tell me how to make this kind of appliqué?

This is appliqué with a difference—actually a reverse appliqué technique. It looks very complicated, but it isn't really difficult to create marvelous "folk art" effects using what is an inlay/onlay process. You may not want to start off with as large a project as a blouse, but you could begin by making some colorful placemats.

For the placemats, you'll need large pieces of felt in several bright colors, matching cotton thread and a No. 4 crewel needle. Select a color and cut it into the size you want for the top of the mat. Fold this in half, then in half again, then once again, the way children do paper cutouts. Cut circles and triangles out of this, then open the piece and lay it on another of your pieces of colored felt. Pin it down and cut away slightly smaller shapes on the next layer, so that a narrow border line of the new color shows all around inside each of the shapes you cut in the first piece. Continue layer by layer, color by color, making smaller and smaller shapes, until the final color forms the base of the mat. Hem down each to the next as you go, then bind the edge of the mat with one of the predominant colors.

Felt is easy to work with because you don't have to make turnbacks, although the traditional material is fine cotton. If you do use cotton, you must fold back about three-eighths of an inch all around. Cut little snips in the hems so that each piece will lie flat along the curved lines as you hem it down. Although I ordinarily recommend iron-on Pellon for appliqué work, it won't do here. With all those layers, it would be too thick and stiff.

Background

I've just finished a small design of my family coat of arms in needlepoint. Now I'd like to mount the needlepoint canvas on the linen I have chosen as background. How can I do this so that the needlepoint lies smoothly on the linen?

The first step is to unravel the raw edges of the canvas around your finished work so that single threads poke out straight on all 4 sides. (You did leave enough margin of canvas around the design, I trust!) Pin and baste the needlepoint in position and then, with a large-eyed needle, take each thread down through the linen close against the edge of the needlepoint. Knot the threads together in pairs, pulling snugly. You can leave the edge as it is—it will be neat and even—or edge it with an outline stitch such as chain or back stitch.

I've worked my needlepoint tapestry in the traditional continental stitch. Can you suggest a background stitch to go with it?

A nice textured background, one that would contrast with the smoothness of the continental stitch, can be created with the "random bargello," a series of long and short vertical stitches of varying length. As you can see from the diagram, you first work a row of long and short stitches, each stitch an irregular length. Then fit the next row into the first, again making each stitch an irregular length. Start at the top of your design when you begin the first row. Never go over more than 8 threads of your canvas, and never go over fewer than 3. Always keep the stitches straight up and down; it should be easy once you set the first few rows in perfect vertical order.

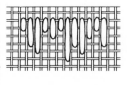

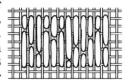

Background

*My mother always used a basket weave stitch
for the background of her chair covers. Isn't
this a waste of yarn?*

Not at all! Things that get a lot of wear need
the extra strength. As you can see from the
diagram, the basket weave stitch is extremely
strong on the back. Because you always go
down into the same holes of the previous
stitches, it's easy to work large areas very
smoothly with the basket weave — another
reason the stitch is ideal for backgrounds.

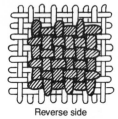
Reverse side

Back of Canvas

*The cross stitches I worked on an evening
skirt are lovely on the front side but the back
is a scramble. How can I avoid this?*

Work your cross stitches in rows as much as
you can. This way you can take a straight repeating stitch on the reverse side. When you
do have to jump, conceal your stitches in the
background material by weaving them in. It's
best to work out your pattern in advance so
you don't have to jump far from one place to
another, avoiding that backside scramble.

Back Stitch

*Just from looking at it, I would have thought
the back stitch is easy to master. I was wrong!
Can you give me some hints?*

The back stitch is easy in theory, harder in
practice, mainly because all the stitches must
be exactly the same size. Following the diagram, come up at A, then go down at B, then
up ahead at C. Repeat, going back into the
same hole as the previous stitch.

Bargello

I've seen your "kaleidoscope" bargello pillow design and would love to create my own, but I don't think I'm equipped to do it.

The only "equipment" you'll need is a mirror — and your native talents. Give it a try! Kaleidoscope bargello lets you carry your favorite bargello design around the 4 corners of a square. Just place 2 mirrors at right angles to one another on a bargello design. By shifting the angle, you can create new shapes and see what the finished effect will be.

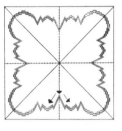

First fold your canvas in half and then in half again, creasing the folds. Open it and mark the lines with a sharp pencil. Place the canvas on a table. Kneel so that you are at eye level and then move the canvas until you can see the diagonal lines clearly. Lay a ruler beside the diagonal that bisects the center and mark this with a soft-tipped marker. Repeat on the opposite side. You'll begin on the slice of pie that's to the right of the diagonal, stitching regular bargello across it, then repeating it on the other 3 sides. Start where the arrow indicates on the diagram, and make your peaks and curves (according to your design), going out to the diagonal line and then across to the other side.

It's just like regular bargello—you set your pattern first, work it all the way around the outside, then when you fill in the stitches, work all the color going in toward the center. Start on any of those straight central lines, work out to the diagonal, go back to the center, work out to the diagonal and repeat exactly on the other 3 sides. When you get up to a diagonal with your stitches, go down exactly on the diagonal line to make those lovely, clear lines of demarcation on the indentations. Notice that both sides will share the holes on that diagonal — the real secret!

Bargello

I'd like to start on a bargello project, but I am confused about how to work the stitch. Can you describe it?

The essence of bargello is its flat, smooth effect and, of course, the brilliant variations you can work by changing a single color or stitch within your overall pattern. Remember that in bargello you always work with the shortest stitch possible on the reverse side. Notice, in the diagram here, that if you pass over 4 threads on the front, pick up only 2 on the back. Only when blocks of stitches are worked side by side should you carry the needle across the back, coming up on one side and down on the other, like satin stitch. Note that when the line of stitching slants upward, the needle slants down. In order to maintain a short stitch at the back, the process is reversed on the way down, when the needle slants upward. Short stitches at the back are essential; they prevent the finished project from looking bulky.

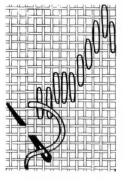

Bedspreads

I want to embroider a bedspread, but I am reluctant to tackle such a large design on my own. Are there are any predesigned kits?

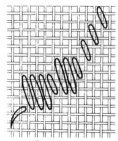

Reverse side

Finding a crewel bedspread kit would probably be difficult. Because people have such a wide variety of bedroom decoration schemes, manufacturers can't sell predesigned kits in large enough quantities to make it worthwhile. But you might do what I do — join crewel pillow squares together for a fun, "portable" coverlet project. You can appliqué the squares onto a background or perhaps join them in checkerboard fashion, using the backing as the alternate "solid" square.

Black Work

I've just seen the most beautiful sixteenth century costumes, all decorated with formalized flowers, silhouettes and intricate designs. What is this work called?

You've just been introduced to black work, an elaborate form of embroidery done in black (and sometimes gold) threads on cream-colored linen. Black work is fine, delicate and sophisticated, so the secret of any design is in getting the right balance of the dark, light and medium areas. It must be done on evenly woven material, because part of its effect is in working geometric stitches to fill the different areas of the design, using a monochromatic color scheme. (The most important thing is to find a material with clear, even weave, because all the stitch patterns have to be counted on the background, following the mesh of the threads.)

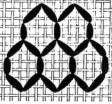

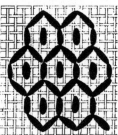

Finished effect

Fine fingering knitting wool, Dacron fiber or fine tapestry wool are all good threads. For finer effects, use a 6-strand mercerized cotton embroidery floss or sewing silk. For the interspersed gold work, try Lurex, the gold twine that is often used for Christmas packages. Use blunt tapestry needles in a size to correspond with the thickness of your wool and your background fabric.

Patterns for black work are necessarily stylized, but you can begin with simple silhouette shapes, filled in with different lacy patterns, worked close or openly. I'm sure you're familiar with the 3 basic stitches: cross, back and running. Try a pattern based on back stitch, which suddenly becomes a honeycomb! Make a series of slanting back stitches over 2 threads from A to B. Work vertical stitches over 2 threads from C to D. Complete the honeycomb, then work a single vertical stitch over 2 threads in each center.

Black Work

I've kept the main area of my black work design very open and airy. But now that I've finished, I feel it needs a denser pattern, perhaps as a border. What would be an appropriate stitch?

Let me introduce you to squared filling—I'll show you the basic pattern for this most versatile stitch, and in no time at all you'll be discovering all kinds of variations. And you'll notice that you can vary color as you go. How fortunate that your basic design is open; squared filling looks best set off by plain surroundings.

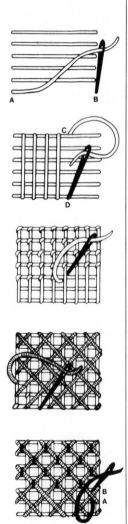

To begin, come up on one side of the shape, make a long stitch right across, go down. Continue until you've filled the shape with exact parallel lines, ¼ inch apart. Now lay threads in the opposite direction. Tie down these squares at the corners. Using a contrasting color, diagonally crisscross the whole design with long lines, first in one direction across the center of every other square, then in the other direction, so that the threads cross in the center of the basic square. With another contrasting color, tie down these diagonal lines where they cross in the center of the squares. This stitch should touch the basic squares at the top and bottom.

Now try a variation, using a blunt needle. After the parallel lines are down in one direction, go across in the other, but weave under and over the way you do in darning. Starting across the broadest part, with contrasting color, pick up the first threads diagonally at the intersection, but do not sew through the fabric. Work diagonally across to the bottom, then upward. Do not pull too tightly. Leave one intersection clear, but weave another diagonal line down the next, using a contrasting color.

I've done a sampler of black work stitches, and I even experimented with the same stitch in different thicknesses of wool, as you explained. But now I would like to work on some table linen. What kind of design do you suggest I use for this?

That is a question! Since your linen is probably going to get a good deal of wear, you might want to try to stick to the simpler, flatter stitches, avoiding the raised and padded stitches. Something as simple as the darning stitch in black against a snowy white linen background can be very exciting just because of its simplicity. You could use the darning stitch, in diamond-shaped rows, to create borders around the table linens.

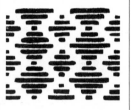

Use a blunt needle and a thread about the size of your linen, weaving horizontal lines across the fabric, as in the diagram. Your first row is made by coming up, going over 7 threads, then down and under 3 threads, then up and over 7, continuing along the line. On the next line immediately below, come up 1 thread in and go over 5 threads, under 2, over 1, under 2, and over 5 again. Repeat along the line. On the next line, come up 1 thread in from the line above and go over 3 threads, under 2, over 3, and under 2. Now repeat the steps in descending order above the first line to form the diamond pattern.

Once you have mastered the technique of counting — and you have the even weave of your linen to help you with that—you'll find that you can work marvelous variations, such as rows of alternating long and short stitches or zigzags that look like bargello stitch. Of course, you may already have decided to weave gold threads into your black work patterns, in which case you need one word of caution: if your gold threads are tarnishable, don't wet the fabric but press the design face downward into Turkish toweling, using a damp cloth under the iron.

Blocking

I just love to do needlework, but oh, how I hate that blocking! Isn't there some kind of shortcut method?

For those of you with a block about blocking, here's good news—a gift from our other artist friends. It's stretcher strips. Yes, those precut strips of wood (they come in all sizes) that have mitered edges which fit together to create a frame on which artists stretch their canvases.

Here's how you can use them for every kind of work — needlepoint, crewel embroidery, and crewelpoint, whether your stitches are flat or raised. You start by putting 4 staples at the 4 corners of the frame, pulling your needlework straight and taut as you put in the staples with one of those heavy-duty staple guns. Gradually add more staples, pulling the fabric or canvas tight with a pair of pliers or someone's helping hand. But don't staple all of one side! Work out gradually from your 4 central staples, adding staples from side to side until you end up with a staple about every ¼ inch.

Now for the real surprise—off to the showers! Tub, actually, where you will run water over your needlework, wash it gently if it is soiled, and then prop it up and let it dry. What could be a more convenient, practically one-step method of blocking and cleaning and drying? And your work will dry so much faster than if you had tacked it to a board where the air could not circulate all around and through it. And this method eliminates one of those questions I am asked constantly: Do I block face down or face up? Now you can block "standing up," saving face completely! I hope this new method will reconcile you to blocking once and for all, for nothing else gives your finished work such a fresh look.

Brick Stitch

I remember reading somewhere that brick stitch is basically a satin stitch. But how can such different textures be so closely related?

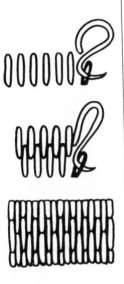

A "satin" stitch isn't really a stitch, but simply the result of laying threads side by side to cover an area closely. When you do a brick stitch, you are doing exactly that, but in a pattern that resembles rows of neat and orderly bricks—which is of course the secret of this kind of stitch. As you can see from the diagram, you work one row with the space of one thread between each stitch. Work a second row so that the stitches overlap halfway into the previous row. Then you work the third row so that the stitches come up into the lower hole formed by the first row of stitches. The finished effect is a row of bricks that lie as smooth as satin!

Bunka

I'm interested in a Japanese form of stitchery called "Bunka." I hope you have heard of it because many stores I've gone to haven't!

Bunka is done with a special hook and a knubby, fine, mercerized cotton thread (a bouclé). If you work on a fairly fine linen, you can get the knack of it, which is similar to rug hooking. Because the thread has such a "bouclé" effect (springy and wiry, like unraveled knitting yarn), it forms little bunches on the reverse side. Because these bunches stay in place, the back of the design looks like a thick mat of hooked loops. The front has a smooth, long-and-short blended appearance, which seems realistic and yet has a certain watery, impressionistic effect — and what could be more Japanese?

Buttonhole Stitch

I've just looked closely at the marvelous embroidery on the shawl I recently bought in Mexico —and the stitch looks just like a buttonhole stitch. Can this really be the stitch that was used?

The buttonhole as transformed by some rather ingenious fingers, I'll bet! Borders, flowers and lacy work can all be created by easy variations on one of the oldest and most practical of stitches. Last spring I did a handbag using the flowers from my garden as inspiration. I outlined the pansies and peonies in the buttonhole stitch, with the loops toward the outside edge of the petals, and then proceeded inward toward the center of the flower with the long and short stitch.

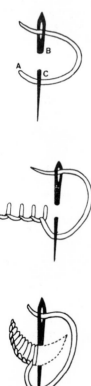

But why not try a design of your own? The buttonhole stitch, as shown in the diagram, begins with the needle coming up at A, then down at B, up again at C, which is directly below B and level with A. The thread is held under the needle. In the second step, you'll see that the next stitch repeats the first at an even distance. You may want, however, to work your stitches closer together, as shown in step 3. Notice how different the effect is here — slightly curved and crescent shaped. This is, of course, only the beginning! Circles, squares and geometrics are only a few buttonhole stitches away. The stitch could even be a pivotal point for another stitch—the way I used it in my spring flower handbag.

And, of course, consider the variations you can achieve by using wools of different thicknesses. While you're at it, you might return to one of the original uses of the stitch— to bind the raw edges of blankets so they won't fray. From the look of some old coverlets that are still around today, women did extensive experiments with colors and textures — making fancy stitches out of handy ones.

I would like to add some variations to the usual buttonhole stitching I do around my blanket edges. Do you have some suggestions for me to try?

Variation is at times the soul of all fine needlework. One variation of the buttonhole I love (even though it does remind me of chicken feet!) is done this way: work 1 slanting stitch, 3 straight stitches and 1 more slanting stitch in a block together; then leave a space, work the next block and stitch all around the edge of your blanket. You could also work straight blocks of 3 stitches in a close group, leave a space, work a block of 2 stitches, leave another space, then work 3 stitches and so on. I'm sure you've already found out how perfectly the buttonhole lends itself to a circle, with the loops facing outward. You could start in the middle, taking all your stitches into one central hole, then work widening rings around the circles, using the blocks of 3 patterns.

Far be it from me to challenge an expert, but I don't think your "buttonhole" stitch looks at all like the one that most tailors use for making buttonholes.

I'm not challenged — I'm corrected, and justly so! I've adopted a lazy needleworker's habit about names, forgetting that the stitch I really mean to talk about is the "embroidery" buttonhole or the "blanket" stitch. The real buttonhole is, as you know, the "tailor's" buttonhole — that beautiful hand-stitching seen on the buttonholes of expensive suits. As you can see from the diagram, the stitch requires perfect, even stitches that lie slightly spaced apart, like little twisted loops in a straight, even row. Not easy work, I assure you, and I can't count the tears I've shed when my loops waved up and down like the lines on a temperature chart!

Canvas

What kind of needlepoint canvas is best for the set of dining room chairs I want to do?

Since you have to buy canvas by the number, I'd better begin by explaining how canvas is calibrated and sold. First of all, the number always refers to the number of mesh threads to an inch. For example, a No. 18 canvas has 18 threads to an inch; a No. 7 has 7, and a No. 12 has — guess! But to answer your question: Choosing the right kind of canvas really depends on the effect you want to create with your needlepoint. If you use a No. 18 canvas, you'll have 18 threads to an inch, and a very delicate effect. You'll find 12 to 14 is a good average, and 7 is quite bold.

The edges of my canvas keep unraveling. What do you suggest I do?

If you've started and haven't bound the edges of your canvas, stop and do it today! I bind my canvas with masking tape, which is fast and inexpensive. Iron-on seam binding is good, but you might also use hand-sewn binding.

Sometimes the canvas I buy is too stiff and sometimes it's too soft. How do I deal with these extremes?

Either way it's a problem, but the stiffer a canvas is, the poorer its quality. The stiffness comes from the sizing a cheap canvas needs to hold its shape. Examine a canvas closely, passing up those with threads that seem rough and hairy. If your canvas is stiff, try working it between your hands. The best thing for a limp canvas is to work it in an embroidery frame. The best canvas today is imported from France or Germany.

I've read about something called "plastic" canvas, but I'm a little reluctant to ask for it in a store. It sounds sort of cheap and tacky – is it especially good for some projects?

Well, my husband calls it "space-age" canvas, and it does have wonderful possibilities for a wide variety of quick, easy and charming projects. It's great for those needleworkers who don't like to do blocking, because it is stiff enough not to need it, and yet flexible enough to be worked in hand or in a frame. It also doesn't fray, so you can cut right along the edge where your stitches stop. No turning back or finishing is needed. Plastic canvas is perfect for three-dimensional projects like pocketbooks, Christmas tree ornaments and book covers. The canvas has clear squares, and your stitches will zoom along, especially when you use your needlepoint frame. Just take the outer ring off a standing or fanny frame and lash the plastic canvas to the inner ring by oversewing it with big stitches. It is available in precut pieces and now is also sold by the yard in 10 or 5 mesh. So why not have some fun with a delightful innovation?

I used too many threads of yarn and then had to cut out some stitches. Now I have to repair the canvas I accidentally snipped while doing this. Can you tell me how?

All is not lost, and repairs are not all that difficult. Fill the canvas with stitches all around the hole, leaving one-half inch of open space. Then ease the broken threads to the back and weave them into the stitches. (Since the ends of the canvas will be short, you'll have to first push the needle into position and then thread it.) Unravel 2 or 3 long threads from the canvas edge, and darn these into the hole (working on the reverse side). When you're all finished, you'll have a perfect and completely invisible repair job!

Cathedral Windows

I'd love to do a patchwork quilt in the cathedral window pattern. I warn you, I'm just a beginner, so can you show me the steps?

You've picked one of the most beautiful patterns — worth the time to master a few major points. Follow the diagram closely and, because the finished folded square will be ¼ the size you started with, use graph paper as a pattern in cutting your cloth.

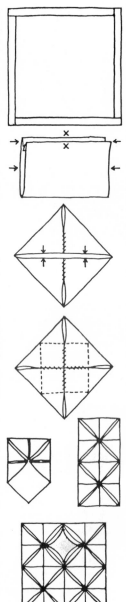

Step 1: Fold back ½-inch turnbacks all around. Step 2: Fold in half and stitch each side together between the arrows. Then pull open at the crosses and flatten in the diamond shape. Step 3: Stitch together between the arrows; be careful not to catch the back of the fabric. Step 4: Fold each of the 4 points back to the reverse side (fold on the dotted line in the diagram). Step 5 (the folding-in process): Catch all 4 flaps firmly together in the center, again careful not to catch the back of the fabric. Step 6: Join the squares. You must join at least 4 squares before you can form your first window. Step 7: Cut out a diamond of contrasting fabric the exact size of the shaded area (plus turnbacks). Catch it in place, then fold back the 4 edges of the original fabric to form a rolled border overlapping the contrasting diamond all around. Hold the rolled edges in place by catching them together at the 4 corners for a three-dimensional effect.

Repeat these steps with different fabrics on each of the other diamonds. That's all there is to it! And once you've collected lots of these diamonds, join them by stitching all firmly together at the 4 corners. (The pattern forgets it is made of diamonds and turns out looking like interlocking circles.) Try backing your diamonds with an interesting contrasting fabric or keep the air spaces open for a lovely, light and lacy bedspread.

Cathedral Windows (quick)

I've heard about an old (but quick) method of making cathedral windows. Have you?

Yes, I confess I have, and it is a rather well-kept Victorian secret. Draw a circle (with the bottom of a glass) onto paper and cut it out. Fold it in half and in half again, giving you 2 straight edges and 1 curved one. Turn back the curved edge so you have a triangle. Now cut through all the layers, using the curved edge as a guide. When you open the paper pattern, you'll have a cathedral window diamond. Lay this down on your fabric and trace around the outline. Machine-stitch bias binding along the pencil lines, trim it around the edges of the bias, turn the tape back and hem on the wrong side. Join the diamonds with oversewing and a lovely lacy pattern will be formed. Mount this on another fabric so a contrasting color will shine through the "windows."

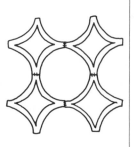

Chain Stitch

I always seem to get one of those "weak links" when I do a row of chain stitches — a tiny gap shows at the point of some stitches. Why does this happen?

People must be afraid that the stitch will just pull out of the fabric if the needle goes back into the same hole twice — and that's your problem! Begin by coming up at A (in the diagram), form a loop, put the needle in at A *again*, holding the loop down. Come up at B, directly below A, and draw through, forming a chain. Repeat, always inserting the needle exactly where the thread came out, *inside* the last loop — come up directly below, and draw through so that the chain stitches lie flat on the material. No weak links!

Chatelaine

My mother says the reason I do my needle-work so slowly is that I'm always looking for things — my scissors, or my thimble. How do I keep track of the things I need?

A chatelaine! Your pins and needles, scissors and thimble won't wander when they're attached to a long ribbon and worn around your neck — and a yard of grosgrain ribbon, marked off in inches, can also double as a decorative tape measure. One end of the tape can have a little felt pocket for a thimble and a pincushion, the other carries your scissors. Chatelaines make wonderful gifts.

Children Needleplayers

My 6-year-old is fascinated by my crewel embroidery and, naturally, wants to do her own. How can I get her started on a project?

Never too early, I say — so start your daughter on some basic stitches. Buy some of those crayons that you iron on, making them permanent transfers to your fabric. Your little student can try some touches of embroidery in combination with the crayons, adding French knots, and buttonhole, couching and puffy couching stitches. The couching stitch is great fun because a child can take thick bundles of thread and stitch them down with finer stitches. Puffy couching creates wonderful hair and animal tails because you leave the bundles of thread in loose loops between the stitches. Random couching makes a perfect wiggly worm or some beautiful tails for frisky horses. Start your daughter off right with an embroidery frame with a support. With the fabric stretched flat, she can "paint" with her stitches just the way most children like to do with their crayons.

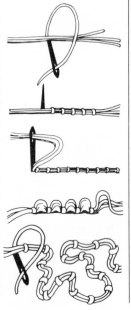

I've just volunteered to teach an arts and crafts class for children in a neighborhood program (ages kindergarten through sixth grade). I think needlework would be so much better than the usual crayon and cut-ups. Could you give me some tips?

Three cheers for you and your program! If we'd all take a closer look at those magnificent samplers (museum treasures today) done by children in the seventeenth and eighteenth century, we'd realize how creative "unprogrammed" youthful minds and fingers can be.

I'm convinced that plastic canvas was invented for children. It's safe, it's stiff enough to cut up into shapes, and it doesn't need any finishing off. With plastic canvas your kids can use blunt needles — no accidents here! Remember, when threading the needle, knot a double strand of yarn. That way, when your pupils pull with great gusto as they stitch, you won't have to rethread every minute — saving you a lot of needless footsteps and frazzled nerves!

As far as individual projects — anything goes, but I'd suggest, from experience, that it's best to make them short and sweet. So how about a row of plastic canvas needlepoint houses? A little community action would do well here, with each child making a separate wall, for example. Assembling the finished parts could be as gala an occasion as one of those famous early American barn-raisings or a twentieth-century "topping off" ceremony — even skyscrapers are topped off!

The diagram shows how simple it is to assemble your plastic canvas. And why not set them to do projects they can take home as gifts? Eyeglass cases, toaster covers, telephone book covers — these are just a few of the things that can be done quickly on plastic canvas, and they are assembled easily. Not only that — they look dashing!

Finished effect

Cleaning Your Needlework

I do a lot of embroidery —always in a frame, as you recommend. Now, after a week or so, I've finished stitching, and the hoop has left a dark, noticeable circle. What can I do?

First of all, always remove the hoop when you're not stitching. That's the ounce of prevention you need. If you must leave the hoop on, put your work in a pillowcase so that loose dirt can't settle on it. If you're using a plastic hoop, you should wrap the inner ring with bias tape first. If you're stitching on delicate material (silk, velvet), put some sheets of tissue paper over the material in the inner ring, then lay the outer ring over, tearing the paper away, leaving a nice padding.

I've spent a whole year on a needlepoint design, and now that I'm about to block it, I see it has suffered from so much handling. What can I do about the dirt marks?

Praise the day the stretcher frame was invented! Buy two pairs of stretcher strips at an art supply store. Staple the needlepoint evenly and tightly around the frame, then hold it under cold water; rub mild soap into the back of the canvas and rub gently. Daisy fresh!

You can also freshen up a crewel pillow by stapling it to your stretcher strips, then washing it. Because the fabric is held out square by the frame, washing won't crush the stitches against one another and the background fabric will stay crisp and even. As it dries, the fabric shrinks within the frame, giving a wonderful smooth finish to your work. As an extra precaution, place the staples in the turnback, or bury them close beside the piping of a finished pillow; then if one strays onto the front it will not mark the linen.

26

My dining room chair seats were worked in needlepoint 25 years ago. They are soiled, and I'm afraid to clean them. What can you recommend that will not damage them?

There are a few possibilities, but first you may want to consult your local dry cleaner for his professional advice. I don't recommend removing the covers and wetting them. They are bound to change shape, and you'll have a problem getting them back on the chairs — and the creases will show all those years of wear! You might try one of those home dry-cleaning sprays, being careful not to soak the fabric. You then brush or vacuum the spray off. And here's an old (English!) home remedy: rub dry white bread lightly over the surface of the seat covers. Those colors have mellowed over 25 years, so don't expect them to look new again — just clean!

Is there any way for me to clean the two old quilt tops I found in a relative's attic?

If they are very frayed or worn, you can be assured they're not going to take like a duck to water. But if they look strong, throw them into the washing machine. Yes, the washing machine! This will save your quilt from the strain of pulling it from a basin while it's heavy with water. Let the quilt soak for an hour, after you've added a mild detergent to the machine. Turn the knob to spin dry, then to rinse, then to spin again. You may have to repeat these steps up to 7 or 8 times until the water in the rinse cycle comes absolutely clean. That's a must; otherwise when the quilt is hanging to dry, streaks of dirty water will appear — and stay. Be sure to test for color fastness. Wet some blotting paper, dab it on the bright colors and see if they come off (if the quilts were made before 1850, you can assume the colors won't run).

Color and Your Needlework

After months of work, I've just finished a project – and it's all wrong! Not the design or the stitches themselves, but the colors. I need help, but how can you help me on something as personal as color preferences?

You're right — color is so personal! But let me tell you what happened in my student days at the Royal School of Needlework in London. For my first sampler I went wild and picked one of each color — and wound up with a sampler that spelled mass confusion. My neighbor did hers in variations of green and created a magnificent piece because of this restraint. Now I always choose my colors beforehand, gathering a bunch of delicious-looking skeins together as if they were flowers. I add or eliminate by holding extra colors beside the main ones. Always keep in mind that too many loud colors take away from the force of the design, while too many close shadings could make it look muddy.

Isn't there a "science" of color? I'd like to select my colors more carefully than with my usual hit-or-miss method.

There certainly is, and science can help you improve your needlepoint art. The diagram shows a color wheel. Red, blue and yellow are the primary colors. The colors between come from mixing two adjacent colors (red and yellow make orange; yellow and blue make green; blue and red make purple). Therefore, colors next to each other on the wheel blend softly together. Colors opposite each other have the strongest contrast. If you put them together, each will give forth its own intensity and neither will overpower the other. How about trying a little "scientific" mixing for your next design?

1. Red	4. Green
2. Orange	5. Blue
3. Yellow	6. Purple

I've had to stop working on my large floral design needlepoint project — the colors are all wrong. The flower bouquet is in bright and dark colors, but the paler flowers almost disappear against the beige background.

Your problem began, I think, when you selected a neutral color like beige as a background. A good test is to half-close your eyes and look at the colors of your flowers and leaves. If the overall tone of the design is pastel, you need a harmonious but deeper background shade. I generally like a beige that is deep enough to let white show up against it. Then, you can always highlight the edges of petals, starting with white and blending into deeper tones. To rescue your disappearing petals, the best thing would be to take a single thread of slightly deeper color and back stitch the outline all around. Work the canvas as though it were embroidery linen to get a nice smooth back stitch that looks like a finely penciled outline.

What do I do when I discover that half a thread of the painted canvas design I am following is painted one color, half another? I get confused and don't know what color is supposed to go in what hole.

Your confusion can really pay off this time, because your canvas is painted the best way — one that gives you a chance to follow the freely drawn curves of a design, rather than the rigid, "stepped" lines. Just disregard the mesh altogether and work spontaneously with your needle. You'll never make the mistake of taking an abrupt "step" when changing color. Take each section of a curve with gradual changes of color for a natural look. Work all main outlines first, background later. Then look it over and add stitches to improve your lines.

Cording

Is there a simple way for me to make my own cording to finish off pillows I've worked?

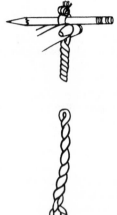

As simple as the time it takes — along with a doorknob (or a willing friend) and a pencil. First, knot 2 single lengths of wool together at each end and double the length you want the finished cording to be. Secure one end to your friend or doorknob. Insert the pencil through the knot at the end, and twizzle the pencil round and round until the wool begins to "kink." Once this happens, hold the wool taut, fold the length in half, allowing the wool to twist back on itself. Stroke it to make it smooth and knot the open end. With a single strand of the same wool, stitch the cord to the edge of your pillow with slanted stitches that are concealed in the cording. (I've been told you can even twist with an egg beater!)

Counting

My geometric needlepoint design will involve a lot of counting. On your television show, did you advise counting threads or the holes in the canvas?

Always think positive—which means you count what's there, the threads, and not what isn't, the holes. And while you're counting, run your needle along parallel with the threads of the fabric to keep things accurate. Try to think of your needlepoint canvas as a piece of tightly woven linen, with no holes between the threads. This will bring a certain logic to things, and you'll never wonder, halfway across a line, if you're about to go into the fifth hole or the fourth thread. After a while, you should become so adept at counting off that you'll do it without a single hitch.

Crewel

I think I'm suffering from a case of not being able to see the forest for the trees! I just looked at a book of crewel embroidery stitches and I am dumbfounded by the sheer number. Can you reduce this to some order?

I do sympathize with someone taking a first look at the possibilities of crewel stitches. But take heart — all those stunning variations actually stem from a handful of basic stitches. I like to call these the Adams and Eves of all the others — stem, satin, chain, cross, back, weaving and filling. I'll tell you a little about each: STEM stitch is probably one of the oldest in the world, although its early form is scarcely distinguishable from weaving. It's equally effective used as a single outline or in rows that fill an area solidly. The next logical development from the stem is the SPLIT stitch, where the needle splits through the thread instead of coming up alongside it. Next comes SATIN stitch, not really a stitch at all! Here threads are laid side by side to closely cover an area. In CHAIN stitches, loops of thread are drawn through one another to make a chain, which is stitched on fabric. CROSS stitches may be worked separately or close together to fill an area. BACK stitch probably has its origin as the very strongest way of holding two pieces of cloth together — it is the stitch the sewing machine does for you! WEAVING stitches are as old as fabric itself. Weaving can be done on the surface, or woven into existing fabric. Last are the FILLING stitches, most of which cover an area with geometric patterns. You can fill silhouette shapes with these stitches or add them to create those "special" effects that are so exciting in embroidery—tactile, three-dimensional areas in your design. In no time you'll learn how to blend your stitches.

Crewel

My husband used to call it my "cruel" work, because it took me a few desperate tries to get the knack of it. He's kinder now, but I am ashamed to admit I actually don't know what the word means.

Impress your husband with your erudition — if he should ask. Crewel probably comes from the Anglo-Saxon word *cleow* (later *clew*), meaning a ball of thread. So you see, when we talk about crewel we are really referring to yarn, not to a kind of stitch. In fact, none of the stitches used in crewel is exclusively a "crewel" stitch, so it's easy to draw from other kinds of needlecrafts for variety as well as inspiration.

A friend of mine, who never does anything but needlepoint, insists that crewel work is too limited for her. I know she's wrong, but I would like to back up my argument with some ammunition from an expert.

You can "hit" her with this one: if crewel is so limited, why have people been doing it since about the fourth or fifth century A.D.? She might have heard that crewel can only be done on linen. Linen is traditional, but any material that's firmly woven and whose threads are easily separated by a needle is just as good. (Of course, light cottons like muslin or percale are inappropriate, since the material will pucker when you use heavy yarn.) And there is no limitation to the kind of wool you can use in crewel: Persian, English or French are perfect, used single thread or with up to 6 strands. And as for stitches — not only can you borrow from every other kind of needlework, but there are scores of variations possible, working just from a handful of basic stitches. If that's limitation ... !

Crewelpoint

When you mentioned crewelpoint I was a bit confused. Is it crewel done entirely on needlepoint canvas, or crewel used as an accent to needlepoint stitches?

Either or both! That's what's so fascinating about this wonderful combination of crewel stitches worked on needlepoint canvas. Use the crewel stitches as a dramatic, three-dimensional accent or use them exclusively to cover the canvas. In both cases, you can use the regular canvas mesh to keep your stitches even while you count them, while at other times you can treat the canvas as though it were embroidery linen, stitching along the canvas freely as if it were a background fabric. Crewelpoint was created to broaden everyone's thinking about the possibilities of needlepoint, so have fun. But remember, be selective; too many colors ruin the effect.

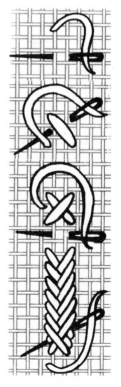

I heard about your invention, crewelpoint, after I began my needlepoint design. Do you think there is any way I could incorporate some crewel stitches into the Victorian flower arrangement I am working on?

Thanks for the compliment, but I am forced to admit that I didn't "invent" crewelpoint at all — there's a beautiful sample at the Boston Museum of Fine Arts that's been around longer than I!

Why not try a border of close herringbone stitches to finish off your design? The stitch may be worked geometrically, by counting the threads. You can work over any number of threads, as long as the canvas is closely covered. This is only the beginning — any of the crewel, stump work, silk and gold and black and white stitches may be experimented with, working either freely or geometrically.

Cross Stitch

Is there any difference between the cross stitch worked in needlepoint and the one in embroidery?

No, the stitch is the same for both, but it has a different effect. Cross stitch on canvas has a solid look, since every thread of the mesh is covered. Cross stitch embroidered on linen may be lighter and more lacy because you can use less thread. Since cross stitch is geometric and must be counted out on the background fabric, you need an even-weave material, whether it is linen, cotton or needlepoint canvas. It's easiest if you work in rows, starting from right to left, making a row of slanting stitches. If the needle is kept vertical and the stitches are spaced evenly apart, the slant of each stitch will remain the same. Keep the needle vertical when you return along the line from left to right, going into the exact holes of the first row of slanting stitches. Always keep the final stitch slanting in the same direction.

I'd like to work decorative cross stitches across a blouse top, but my fabric is fine cotton, too fine to count threads. What do you suggest I do?

First work out your design on graph paper, each square in the appropriate color. Baste some mono canvas or scrim to the blouse where the design area is to be. Working in a frame, stitch your pattern right through the canvas and the blouse fabric, counting the pattern as you go. When it's finished, cut the canvas close around the design and ravel out the threads. You'll be left with a beautiful cross stitch design worked on the fine fabric — and everyone will wonder how in the world you managed to do it.

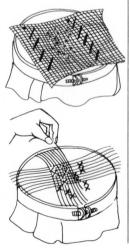

Design

I've never been one of those beginners who begins by beginning, if you know what I mean. What I mean is, I'd like some general guidelines before I create my own design.

I do know what you mean — but it is so hard to be specific when needlework offers such an endless array of possibilities. The entire spectrum of geometric and counted patterns is there for you to choose from, especially if you don't rate your draftsmanship very high. Equally endless is the variety of freehand designs that can be created, right on the canvas or fabric. Always remember the materials you are working with — fabrics, yarns and textures. These do impose limits, so a good rule of thumb is: Will this design look more beautiful in needlework than in any other medium? Always ask yourself what is the essence of the design. If it's light and delicate, then crewel or silk might be best. If the emphasis is on brilliant, solid, overall masses of color, needlepoint is probably your best choice. If it's both — there's crewelpoint!

Enlarging Your Design

It's been some time since I was in school, but I vaguely remember being taught to enlarge a picture by squares. Can you tell me how?

You've almost got it! The method is a simple and inexpensive way to create a design in the size you want. Simply draw small squares on tracing paper on top of your small design, then draw the exact number of squares in larger scale on another piece of tracing paper. Working on this larger grid, you can easily draw your design, copying each section, square by square.

Drawn-Thread Work

The table linens I inherited have drawn thread borders – beautiful, but I don't think I can duplicate them. Is there a technique with a bolder, more modern approach?

Drawn-thread work is an old art that has won many new admirers — especially since we are discovering that instead of fine linen you can use needlepoint canvas (yes, canvas!) with exciting results. You can make colorful pillows with needleweaving or rely on texture for your effect and work entirely in white. A white linen blouse with bands of drawn work down the sleeves or across the yoke would be stunning.

The technique is the same for linen or canvas. First, you determine the width and the length of the border you want, then draw 1 thread out of the linen on either side of it (at AB and CD). Then work a band of buttonhole stitches between A and C, with loops facing inward toward the border. Then work a second band at the other end. Next cut a vertical line between A and C (at arrows), carefully cutting each horizontal thread (not the upright, vertical ones). Repeat this at the other end, cutting close against the buttonhole stitching. Draw out the threads, one by one, until the border is composed only of vertical threads. Now you begin to secure the vertical threads of the border by hemstitching. Using a blunt tapestry needle, come up at A, just underneath the border. Slide the needle under a bundle of 2 or more threads (from B to C). Wrap around these threads and slide the needle into the fabric again at D. Pull tight, then hemstitch the opposite side of the border. Either hemstitch the same group of threads to form a ladder effect, or split the groups, taking one bundle from one group and one from another, hemstitching them together on the opposite side.

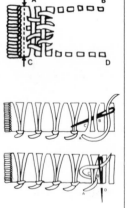

Frames and Hoops

I know you always advocate using a frame when working on crewel embroidery, but I've been told you should never use one for needlepoint. How can I maneuver my large canvas as I work?

You probably expect my answer — in a frame, that's how! Although some hoops are not strong enough for a canvas (the spring-loaded hoops), you can get a wood or plastic frame that has an adjustable screw so that you can stretch your canvas taut. You'll be better off with a frame on a support or stand so that you can work with both hands, one above and one below the frame. For your large canvas, try a square frame, one designed to let you roll up the part you're not working on, then roll up what you have finished. Shall I add some other advantages — like always having your design facing you and being able to keep a few threaded needles of different colors at your fingertips.

So I gave in and used a frame, and now all my lovely raised crewel stitches are squashed by the wooden hoop! May I throw it away now?

By no means! But next time remember that certain delicate materials and raised stitches can be marked by a hoop. To avoid this, place layers of tissue paper over the design, then push the frame down and tear the paper away, leaving a protecting layer around the hoop. Another solution is to mount a piece of linen into the ring frame and then baste your fabric to the linen on top of the frame, just where the design area is. Work through both layers, then cut the linen away on the reverse side. A square embroidery frame with bars on each side allows you to roll your embroidery nice and tight as you progress in your design.

Frames and Hoops

Did you forget to mention it, or was I not paying attention when you described how to put an embroidery frame off and on?

In any case, repetition is the mother of good habits. First make sure your hoop screw is set at the right tension before you put the fabric on. (It's next to impossible to adjust the screw of the outer ring after it's in place because of the tension.) Now push the outer ring over the fabric and the inner ring as you pull the fabric really tight. To take the frame off, push firmly on your fabric with your thumbs, lifting off the ring at the same time with your other fingers. Don't try to unscrew the screw, even with a pliers, because it will probably be under too much tension to turn.

Should I adjust the screw on my embroidery hoop as I work, or leave the hoop at a set tightness throughout?

If you're not adjusting the screw as you work, you're missing one of the great advantages of a hoop. Your work naturally gets thicker as you add stitches, so loosen the screw as needed.

The material I'm embroidering is so fine, it keeps slipping out of my frame. Should I give up and work it in my hand?

Before you do that, take this hint. Just fold back one or two corners of your delicate fabric and slip the double thickness into the frame. The extra bulk will help keep the tautness. Or get some flat binding, often called "lampshade" tape, and wrap it around the inner ring of your frame to give it a soft padding which will hold your fine material firmly.

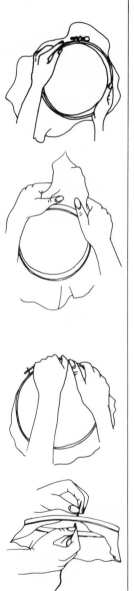

Framing and Mounting

I've finally mastered your crewelpoint, and my finished design is waiting to be framed. But how? Can I just glue it to a piece of wood and leave it at that?

No, never! And for several reasons. Even though many professional framers still use glue on needlework, it could seep through and ruin the work, or bubble and wrinkle the canvas. Frame your work first on the same kind of stretcher strips you blocked it with. First assemble the 4 strips by easing the corners together. Stretch a piece of sheet or muslin over them, securing with staples. Stretch your already blocked canvas over this, pulling so that there are no wrinkles or creases. Secure the canvas with staples and you'll have an absolutely perfect job!

I'm taking my crewel embroidery to have it professionally framed. A friend told me not to use glass over it. But is a picture a picture without a frame and a glass?

In the case of crewel work, it will have to be. Your friend is right; the glass will squash your crewel stitches, and you'll lose the lovely, soft, textural effect you worked so hard to achieve. On the other hand, if you insist on glass, be sure to ask the framer to mount your work with a space between the glass and the fabric, so that the wool stitches are safe. And be wary if your framer suggests nonglare glass. That kind must be pressed tightly to the picture because it has a tendency to distort images if there is even a slight space between it and the work it covers. Again, you know what glass pressed to fluffy crewel stitches will do—flatten out what you worked so hard to make stand up!

French Knots

I wanted a rough-textured foreground for my original crewel design (an abstract, non-representational series of colors and forms). I tried making French knots of different sizes, but they looked so sloppy I ripped them out. Where did I go wrong?

The size of the French knot is determined by the number of threads and the size of the needle used. Were you taking the easy way out and twisting the thread around the needle more than once? Let's follow the diagram: Bring the needle up, twist thread (as many as you want) once around the needle. Put the needle in at or just beside where it came up, pull the thread until it fits closely around the needle, but not too tightly. Then pull the needle through. As the French say: *Voilà!*

I remember from my childhood those dazzling summer fields of sunflowers, so now I'm going to try a needlepainting of what's in my memory. Which crewel stitch would you suggest I use to re-create the spectacular effect of a sunflower?

I'll tell you if you first promise to use your frame or hoop to work the stitch! Nothing will look sloppier than these French knots on stalks if they "flop" all over your painting. To make the stitch, come up at A, and twist the thread once around the needle as in the diagram. Pull gently, so that the thread fits around the needle. Still holding the thread so that it does not loosen, go down at B, about ¼ inch away from A. Pull gently through, to form the effect shown in the diagram. The knots are most effective when radiating from the center of a circle, just like the miraculous burst of those fields of sunflowers you treasure in your memory.

Furniture

I've seen fabulous crewel embroidery wing chairs and bed hangings, and while I'm envious, I'm also somewhat discouraged. Isn't there a furniture project I can do—and still enjoy while I'm hale and hearty?

You could tackle a chair (I did a sofa myself!) and still live to see it completed. But if you want to show your handiwork off in the living room, why not start on something simpler? If you play bridge or backgammon, you have a perfect, "quickie" project. Have a regular playing card blown up by one of those photo-enlarging processes. Card-table size is 33 by 33 inches. Transfer this to canvas, stitch it and bingo (or grand slam!) you're in the living room for good. The sneaky part comes when you fold up the legs and hang the table on the wall as a decorative panel. Backgammon is a terrific indoor sport to translate into stitchery, for the big, flat boards are a natural for every kind of bold design.

And after you've done the living room, move out into the garden and do a needlepoint back and seat for that canvas director's chair. There's a simple way of getting the needlepoint to stick to the chair—and also allowing you to snatch if off when it begins to pour. You've heard of Velcro—those strips of toothed material that adhere to each other. Just attach strips to the underneath edges of your needlepoint canvas and to the top side of the sailcloth canvas of your director's chair. Leaving the original chair canvas in place means that you'll have this extra support under your needlework (no fear of "seat droop"). And you won't have to back the needlepoint canvas that you use for the chair back — the canvas will hide your stitches. And Velcro is so strong the seat and back will not shift, even under the squirmiest child!

Geometric Design

I know you've heard it before: I'm only a beginner, and I know I'll be discouraged if I don't see results at once. . . . Can you suggest something for my first project?

Geometric needlepoint must have been invented especially for you! Let's begin with design — your inspiration can come from countless sources, from stone carvings to peasant costume decorations. As for actually working the design—the even mesh of your canvas makes it easy to count your stitches, beginning in the center of the space and working out to the edges.

I'd like to suggest a pillow made of crisscross lines that form diamonds, which are then filled with either solid or multicolor stitches. To begin, work a double row of tent stitches across the entire canvas in either direction to form diamonds. Work these in either a very light or very dark shade to form a strong contrast with the colors that will fill the diamonds. The diamonds can be in one solid color, or shaded from top to bottom. You can even fill in with a different stitch, such as Algerian eyelet, or even a bargello stitch. Some points to remember about geometric needlework: the simpler the stitch, the more intense the color, because there are no twists or braids to break up the light. Your whole effect becomes different in large or finer scale, so keep this in mind when you lay out your pattern in the beginning. If you have already worked a sampler of needlepoint stitches, you could easily try any one of the stitches to fill in your diamonds. And for a final bonus— you don't have to estimate how much yarn you will need for the whole project and then worry if you'll run out of a particular dye lot. Just make your diamond pillow into a harlequin pattern, so that you'll be using small quantities of different yarns.

Gobelin Stitch

I did a needlepoint tapestry with a Gobelin stitch background because I thought it would be easy. Now the bare threads of my canvas are peeking through even after blocking. What can I do to cover them?

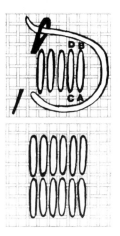

As you can see from the diagram, the straight Gobelin looks like simplicity itself—come up at A, go down at B (4 threads above); then repeat, from C to D, one thread to the left. But if you pull too tightly, spaces will form, showing bare canvas. Now you must work a line of back stitches between all the rows after the area is filled.

Gold Work

I would love to do some "gold work" but, as the saying goes, "I'm a poor working girl!" Do you really use gold?

Heaven will protect the working girl, as the other saying has it. And the perfect gift from heaven is Lurex, a marvelous metallic string (you've seen it on Christmas packages), that has every bit of the luster, and more flexibility, than the original. Because of the flexibility, you can stretch Lurex right through your fabric, not just "couch" it on the surface.

Of course, there is also something called Japanese gold, a thin coating of gold leaf on narrow strips of paper wrapped around a core of silk to form gold thread. It is very beautiful, though delicate, and can only be couched on the surface of your fabric, because putting it back and forth through cloth would spoil it. You can usually obtain Japanese gold through church embroidery supply houses. Using either "gold," you can add glitter to an evening dress, a handbag, or even your husband's cummerbund or vest!

Gold Work

My husband just became president of his sailing club and I want to embroider the club's insignia in gold for his blazer. But I've never worked with gold threads before. Can you tell me what I need and how to use it?

Nothing but the best for the new "commander." "Real" gold can be either bullion threads or Japanese gold—the latter is especially good because it will never tarnish. (Japanese gold is made of pure gold leaf on narrow strips of paper lightly coiled around a core of orange or yellow silk.) Remember that the threads are too delicate to sew right through the fabric, so you have to sew them down on the surface.

Be very accurate in applying your design onto the fabric, stretched in a square frame. To find the center of your area and to give you straight guidelines, baste contrasting colored threads through the middle of the fabric, vertically and horizontally, working between the threads of the fabric with a blunt needle. Almost any kind of couching stitch is perfect for gold work. I'm sure you are familiar with basic couching and the scores of variations on it, such as brick pattern couching and circle couching. Always leave your ends loose on top of the fabric until all the couching is complete. Then "plunge" the ends of the gold through the material with a huge dagger of a  needle (this will protect the gold as it gets pulled through to the back). If the ends are short, first push the needle into the fabric, then thread them one by one, ease them through and cut them off, leaving about ¼ inch ends hanging loose. You probably will not have to block, but press your work face down onto several layers of toweling, cover with a smooth cloth and press with a warm iron—but don't press the loose ends of the gold thread.

I've worked a gold work sampler (fairly expertly, I must admit). Now I'd like to begin another project. Can you suggest one?

Why not dazzle your dinner party with an "envelope" clutch — an oblong handbag as flat as a pancake, patterned after a real envelope. Use ultrasuede or suedecloth, drawing on your design with felt-tipped marker. Try an oriental "wave" pattern — flowing lines of gold thread, couched down with mercerized cotton. The circle couching stitch shown here will create different-sized circles, touched off with a few sequins. Interline your clutch bag with Pellon, line with silk, machine-stitching all around. Fold in three, sew up the sides, edge with gold cord, and end off with an antique button and loop. Beautiful!

Are there any special materials (outside of the gold itself) that I will need to start gold work?

Yes, gold is special, so you'll need a few things, most of which you probably already have: a large (No. 18 chenille sharp or No. 18 needlepoint) needle to open a hole in your background material. When you work one of the delightful couching stitches I have illustrated here you'll see why. The extra-thick ends of the couched threads will pass easily through the back with the No. 18 needle. Be sure to use silk or mercerized cotton thread for couching down. And make sure to "wax" the thread for strength. Get some beeswax (at most notions stores) and thread your needle, drawing the thread two or three times through the wax. The wax makes the thread stiffer and stronger. For background material I recommend fine linen, although you could try rough wool or cotton, or even combine silk, gold and wool when working on damask or brocade. Almost anything goes!

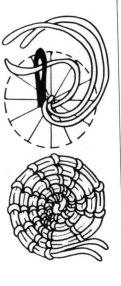

Hardanger Embroidery

I always thought Hardanger was a kind of fabric, but recently I saw a piece of table linen done in beautiful open work that was called Hardanger embroidery. Is the name used for both the fabric and the embroidery?

Hardanger is the name for both the embroidery and the fabric—and if that's not confusing enough, you'll find that today Hardanger fabric is also sold under the name "Aida." Hardanger is a kind of Norwegian white work in which geometric satin-stitch patterns are worked on the even-weave, double-thread Hardanger linen. Open-work fillings are then cut and this drawn-thread-work mesh is strengthened with needleweaving. Because the special double-thread Hardanger linen is so firm, it can be cut close against the satin stitch without fraying.

You can try a sample of Hardanger by first working your geometric pattern in blocks of satin stitches. When you cut away the linen close against the stitching, inside the shape, you leave alternate groups of threads uncut— 2 threads running vertically and 2 threads running horizontally. Then you can begin your needleweaving, working on the reverse side and using a blunt tapestry needle to weave strengthening threads throughout the lattice work you have created by the drawn-thread work. Remember to use fine thread when you are whipping the vertical and horizontal threads of your lattice work together. What you do with your open-work shapes now depends on how many variations of squared filling you want to experiment with. Since squared filling is actually just a basic grid with the intersections tied, you can invent your own method of tying and weaving over the grid. In Hardanger work, your blocks of satin stitch, with their shiny, white look, contrast beautifully with open-work stitches.

Herringbone Stitch

The instruction book I have says, casually, "Make your leaf shapes out of rows of close herringbone stitch." If I knew how, I guess I wouldn't need the instruction book!

First, a refresher course in the close herringbone. As you can see in the diagrams, begin with a cross stitch: come up at A, go down at B (diagonally below A); come up at C, go down at D. Then come up at E, close to A; go down at F, close to B. This will form a solid band of stitching. To work a leaf shape: come up at A (in the leaf diagram), go down at B. Repeat on opposite side (C to D), making 2 closely crossed stitches. Continue working first one side, then the other. Maintain the slant by leaving a space each time you come up (between E and A) and go in close at B. Your finished effect will be lifelike. And it all evolved from the basic herringbone.

Interlaced Herringbone Stitch

I bought a blouse in Greece that is worked on the collar and sleeves with a kind of herringbone stitch, but with threads of different colors run through the basic stitch. Can you tell me how to do this?

The basic herringbone gives rise to so many variations, it's one of the handiest stitches to have around. Your blouse is probably done in the interlaced herringbone. First you work a row of herringbone. Then, beginning on the right, with a blunt needle and contrasting thread, pick up the first bar of the herringbone, slanting the needle downward. Pick up the next bar slanting the needle upward. Continue to the end of the row, being careful not to pull your thread too tight. Once you've mastered this variation you can experiment.

Joining Canvas

My original design was wider than my frame, so I worked it in two pieces, assuming I could just stitch them together. But how?

I hope you haven't completed your project—it's much easier if you leave working threads all down the edges that are to be joined. These will be used to continue the stitching right across the join, once the canvas is stitched together. Crease back the unworked edges (these should be about ½ inch all around). Lay the 2 pieces of canvas side by side, lining up the mesh so that it runs true. Pin them flat side by side and, starting at the top, oversew or whip the threads together, using fine linen or button thread. Join the 2 pieces as though they were one, taking a stitch into each mesh and pulling tightly so that the 2 vertical threads of canvas merge completely together. Hold the 2 turnbacks together on the reverse side and embroider the canvas right across the join, without catching the turnbacks.

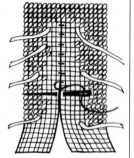

Kits

What should I look for when buying a pre-designed needlework kit?

Look for one of mine, of course! But, seriously, always pick a design you'll keep on loving after working — and looking at — for weeks. Get the best background material — 100 percent linen or cotton (I think rayon is too sleazy). Make sure the canvas has a clear weave, without too many hairy whiskers between the threads. And look for the manufacturer's guarantee that the wool colors are colorfast. Always work in a frame, always block your work when finished and have fun learning and creating, whether you do your own designs or work from a kit.

When I bought my first crewel embroidery kit I loved the design and found that the instructions were easy to follow. But what was left out was how I deal with the simple, practical things—how do I keep all those pieces of yarn organized; where do I begin working on the design? Can you tell me how to use my kit?

Too many "save-time" stitchers (and experienced ones as well as beginners) think they can skip the first step—sorting your wool. But let me warn you—if you don't sort at the beginning, your nerves will be as hopelessly tangled as your yarn! Begin by undoing the bundles of yarn and laying them out on the back of a sofa or a table, each color in its own bundle. Be careful, since some shades are very close.

There are several ways to "file" wool, among them upholstery tape and an old magazine. I find upholstery tape perfect, for wools can be popped in between snaps and held in place. Wooden palettes with holes around the edges are also excellent organizers. Each hole — you could have 5, one for each color range — is threaded with wools, which you draw out easily.

One of the simplest and most inexpensive ways to organize wool is to use an old magazine — label each double spread of the magazine with the number of the wool color, insert the wool and roll up the magazine!

As far as where to start: in needlepoint, work the design first and background later, because your shapes will be clearcut when the background stitches adjust to the stitched shapes. In crewel, work the underneath layers first (stems, then leaves). Do your stitches boldly, because those helpful blue design lines will be unsightly shadows once you're through and haven't covered them completely with your stitches. Remember that those design lines are indelible, and your felt-tipped pen is permanent ink!

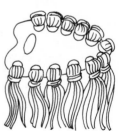

Lace

*Is needlemade lace as impossible as it looks?
I'd love to try a simple piece.*

Not impossible, but not all that simple! Begin
by outlining your design, with double lines,
with a permanent felt-tipped pen, on a piece
of vinyl-coated shelf paper. Now, baste narrow ribbons or machine-made insertion lace
(the kind with a plain edge on both sides)
down within these lines, folding and tacking
them where necessary. Once you decide on
your open-work pattern you'll have to fold or
pleat the ribbons to form smooth curves and
hem them together where they join.

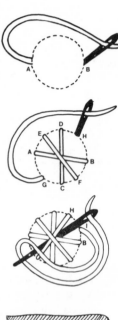

To join the ribbons and form the lace, you
work spider's webs and buttonhole bars, filling the spaces between the ribbons. This is
where the vinyl-coated paper comes in.
When you work the spider's webs, using a
blunt needle and crochet cotton, your needle
will skate across the shiny surface and won't
accidentally pierce through it. Then you can
easily follow the pattern.

The diagram shows a ribbon of lace folded
to form a circle and basted to the vinyl paper.
Work the spider's web inside by criss-
crossing the center (from D to E, F to G, etc.),
concealing the threads by running through
the ribbons as invisibly as possible. When the
whole design is finished, cut the basting
threads to free the lace. Cut on reverse side of
backing to avoid cutting stitches. As well as
filling in between the ribbons with spider's
webs, you can connect them in places with
buttonhole bars. Simply run your thread invisibly into one ribbon, secure it firmly, jump
across to the ribbon to be connected, go back
to the start and then back again to the second
ribbon. This gives you 3 threads across the
join. You now buttonhole stitch back to the
start, closely covering the 3 threads, making a
firm bar.

Lefthanded Needleworkers

We haven't taken to the streets to demonstrate yet, but we lefthanded needleworkers are ready to protest! Why are all directions and diagrams for you righthanders?

I protest! All my needlecraft books insist on working on an embroidery frame or hoop, with a support, so you can use both hands. Since it doesn't matter which hand is on top, you can easily follow the stitches. For the other stitches, why not a mirror? Simply hold it up to the "righthanded" stitches and the instructions will be adjusted to suit you.

Legal Matters

Can I copy crewel designs from a kit I bought? I want to sell them at a church fair.

While the paddy wagon won't pull up at the church door, and while copying once or twice seems safe, individuals can't mass-produce designs that have the protection of the copyright law.

Lettering

I'd like to experiment with needlepointing letters for a contemporary poster wall hanging. What's the best way to proceed?

A good simple block lettering is really the best for needlepoint. Be sure to work out your complete alphabet on graph paper first so that each letter is the same size. Graph paper try-outs let you see if the words will fit in the space you have. Newspapers and magazines can give you all sorts of lettering ideas fit to print, and there are many type manuals and alphabet style books available.

Lettering

I'd like to embroider a sampler, one that spells out my most often repeated "house rules" (the ones most often ignored!). How do I go about spelling out in stitches?

Since you've decided it's time to speak your mind in needlework, here are some basic ABCs. Decide on the kind of type face you want, getting your ideas from type manuals or books, newspapers and magazines, You can even buy sheets of cut stencil alphabets and trace these onto your canvas. If you prefer script writing (for that very personal touch!), then write the words on tissue or tracing paper, baste this to your canvas or fabric, and stitch right through, tearing away the paper when you're finished.

Split stitch or stem are good for script writing, but when it comes to smaller letters, you'll find that the back stitch gives the finest line. Here are some hints: reduce the size of the stitches slightly as you go around curves in letters; it will make them much smoother. Sometimes it is better to overlap one stitch over the other where two lines converge. This makes a sharper point than when you bring both stitches together into the same hole. Be precise about keeping angles clear-cut and straight lines really straight. Sometimes moving a stitch just 1 thread to the left or right can make all the difference — and you want to speak your mind loud and clear! Letters in cross stitch or tent stitch on needlepoint canvas or a fabric with an even weave are simple because they are geometric. Plan them on graph paper first, then, using a blunt needle, you can reproduce them exactly, counting the threads of your canvas or fabric. Whatever style of lettering or kind of stitch you use, I'm sure you will find that the result will be impressive enough to make everyone stop to take a second look—and listen!

Long and Short Stitch

I'm ready to enroll in a course on nothing but long and short stitches! How do I create those flowing lines I admire in other people's crewel flowers and leaves?

Practice — and a few basic principles — will help you do that beautiful long and short soft shading. First draw guidelines on the fabric, then outline the shape with split stitch. Work the first row, as in the diagram, coming up at A and going down over the split stitch at B, starting in the center (or highest point) of each shape. Place the stitches slightly wider on the outside edge and closer in the center, exactly like a fan.

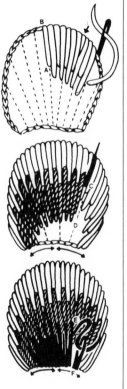

Now work a second row of stitches in the next shade lighter or darker, coming up at C and down at D. Again the stitches fan slightly as in the first row. Stitches should not change direction sharply: have them flow into one another. Split far enough back into the previous row and make the stitches long enough for the third row to split into them. Then, using the third color, fill the remaining space in the center of the shape. Come up at E and go down at F. Bring the stitches evenly down over the split stitch, making a smooth outline as at the beginning.

On the third row it is impossible to fit each stitch exactly back through the previous stitch; every now and again miss one (there is less space in the center of the curve than on the outside). With overlapping shapes, work the underneath one first; start at the tip or farthest from the growing point of flowers, leaves, etc., then work down toward the growing point to keep stitches flowing smoothly. Keep all rows long enough to allow the subsequent stitches to split back into them. "Cheat" with a short wedge stitch along the curve, taking the next stitch very close to it.

Mirrors

I thought it would be nice to do an embroidery frame for a mirror I have. I've done the embroidery—but how do I get it to go around my 12-by-14-inch mirror?

First, the supplies: get some foam core board at an art supply store, masking tape, rubber cement and a "do-it-yourself" frame kit in stainless steel, enamel or plain wood. Block your embroidery, then cut a piece of foam core board to fit it, with a rectangle cut out of the center for the mirror opening. Mount your work on this by first folding back the outer edges around the board, securing them with masking tape. Then, cut 4 diagonal slits from the center to the 4 corners of the mirror opening, cutting ½ inch short of each corner to prevent fraying. Next, fold the 4 flaps to the back of the board, trim them, leaving a hem of 1½ inches, and hold them firmly in place with masking tape. Be sure to stretch tight— no wrinkles, please!

Lay your mounted embroidery on top of a second piece of foam core board and, making sure the two are aligned at the outer edges, run a pencil around the opening for the mirror which is framed by your embroidery. Lift off the embroidery and glue the mirror into position exactly on the marks you have just made on the board, using permanent cement. Finally, with masking tape, hold the 2 pieces firmly together at the edges and frame them in the do-it-yourself frame, following the instructions given.

I'm glad you've tackled your first mirror project, and I know it won't be your last. Not only is a mirror frame a practical idea—just think of the amount of exposure it will give your needlework! And for your next mirror frame, why not try doing your needlework on a plastic canvas—it's stiff and free-standing and doesn't need any backing or turnbacks.

Mistakes

After working for weeks on a crewel embroidery wall hanging, I find I must cut out one huge section of long and short stitches. What's the quickest way to go about it?

Get a pair of curved scissors and cut through all the close stitches on the right side—where the stitches are longer and easier to cut. (The curved scissors will prevent any horrifying snips into your background fabric.) It's much easier to unpick if the whole thing is stretched taut in a frame, because you can scratch away at the cut stitches first on the underside, then on the front to loosen them quickly. With a mistake in needlepoint, you would attack the stitches on the reverse side, where the longer stitches are easier to cut. In that case, too, it's easier to do if your work is in a frame.

Mitering

"Mitering" sounds very regal to me. Does it have anything to do with crowns, scepters, orbs – or maybe archbishops?

Well, certainly the best bed and table linens always have mitered corners, but it's not restricted to royal personages. Actually, mitering is a simple cutting and folding process. As used in needlework, it helps you avoid bulky corners, especially in something like a needlepoint chair cover. You can do it to your blocked needlepoint piece by cutting off the canvas at the corners (at an angle) to within 2 or 3 thread counts of the worked areas. As you fold the sides of the canvas, you'll see what nice, clean edges are formed at the corners because the extra canvas is gone. Another method of mitering is to cut a square of excess canvas for each of the 4 corners.

Needlepainting

I'd like to do one of the "needlepaintings" I heard you talk about. But how do I know what stitches to use?

I'm glad I'm winning converts to this delightful art of painting on fabric with your needle and thread. And you'll be doubly delighted when I tell you that most of the stitches you will use are really just free-form straight stitches, like brush strokes in oil painting. Real "embroidery stitches" aren't necessary and may even give your painting a forced or cluttered look. (Some stitches like French knots and split stitch do prove useful; and I've found that the open buttonhole is great when you want to reproduce brick houses and tile roofs.)

So let's begin! Get 4 of those artist's stretcher strips, assemble them into a frame and stretch your linen very square and taut over it, securing it with a power stapler all around. Begin working the background of your painting first—the hills in the distance, distant trees, etc., gradually working forward to the foreground, so your closer shapes are clear and distinct. This way, you can lay long threads (and long split stitches occasionally) across the sky and work branches of trees, for instance, on top. This method is much easier than trying to fill in little stitches in the background later. Don't be afraid to lay stitches on top of each other—tree trunks over grass, sun over sky, a bee over a flower. To block your painting when you're done, take it (still on the stretcher frame) and run it under the cold water tap of your bathtub. Stand it up to drip, and once it's dry, you'll be amazed at how smooth your stitching comes out. Never skip the blocking step: it will slightly shrink the background fabric and raise your stitches to give them "bounce" and dimension.

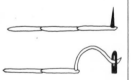

Needlepoint Stitches

I think I had a deprived youth! I always thought there is one kind of needlepoint stitch—the one that covers the canvas. Now I hear there are many stitches. Can you give me a run-down on them?

Now's the time to make up for a misspent youth — and learn the fascinating variety of stitches you can work, even on the regular grid of your needlepoint canvas. TENT stitch is, of course, the usual stitch, and it does give a lovely, smooth, rich effect. But another stitch, the GOBELIN, so closely resembles tapestry that it has been named after the famous tapestry weaving of France since the Middle Ages. ENCROACHING GOBELIN is a close cousin. Its smooth look comes from the blending of the rows — each row of stitches actually projects into the previous row. Another upright straight stitch is BRICK stitch, used for flame stitch or bargello patterns. This stitch is very effective when combined with other stitches in a regular piece of needlepoint. After these upright stitches, CROSS stitches make another separate group with a different effect. There is, of course, simple cross stitch; but also RICE STITCH—a marvelously hard-wearing geometric stitch ideal for rugs. LONG-ARMED CROSS stitch will make borders and rug edgings as well as adding to your design's impact. Turkey work can be cut to form a velvet pile or left in loops to fill a whole design. And, if you'd like more, there's a beautiful stitch called ROCOCO (popular, obviously, in the eighteenth century, the age of the rococo). When worked in small geometric designs, this leaves a pattern of small holes over the canvas. Now, if you want to just stick with the tried-and-true tent stitch, at least you know just how many others you are passing up!

Needlepoint Stitches

I think I'm about to be confused — I may already be confused! I always thought needlepoint stitch was needlepoint stitch. But what is grospoint, and petitpoint, and demipoint? And quickpoint?

Let's begin with what they have in common: *point*. *Point* means stitch in French, so the basic word *needlepoint* indicates that we are dealing with a stitched canvas and not the woven tapestry which it imitates. To go one step more: *petit*, *demi*, and *gros* mean small, medium and large. Now, the basic stitch (which you can do small, medium or large) is called by a great many names: tent stitch, continental stitch, basket weave — even grospoint, demipoint and petitpoint!

Tent stitch is really the only correct name, since all the others describe the different ways of working it. (The word *tent* may really refer to the frame which was always used in working the stitch.) The half-cross or quickpoint stitch is really grospoint, done on very coarse canvas, varying in size from 3 to 7 threads to the inch, using a heavy yarn. The smooth-shading tapestry effect of tent stitch has made this stitch synonymous with needlepoint, but you no doubt are aware of the many other stitches that can give needlepoint variety and excitement.

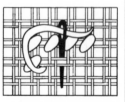

Today, you can even add another "pointed" word to your collection of needlework terms—crewelpoint. This combines the textural effects of crewel with the velvety smoothness of needlepoint. Crewelpoint can be done either by filling in the area with tapestry-like needlepoint stitches and then accentuating the design with crewel textures or by reversing the process, working the background with rows of chain or buttonhole stitch and the design in smooth shading of tent stitch.

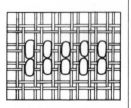

Reverse side

Needles

My question may sound dumb, but could you tell me how to thread a needle with yarn properly?

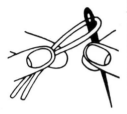

If it's dumb, you're in good company, because it's a question often asked. First, double your yarn over the eye of the needle and pull it tightly, so that the needle practically creases the yarn. Pull the needle away. Then squeeze the thread tightly between finger and thumb. Press the eye of the needle flat onto the thread (don't push the thread through the needle). Remember — squeeze tightly! Knot only one end, leaving the other hanging once it's through the needle.

I tried to buy a packet of needles for my first embroidery project – but what kinds do I select out of hundreds of choices?

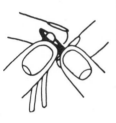

Even experts play eeney, meeney when it comes to choosing a needle. For crewel, many like chenille needles (which have long eyes and sharp points). These come in numbers— the higher the number, the finer the needle, with No. 8 the finest, No. 5 about average. Tapestry needles, with their blunt tips, are good for needlepoint and all stitches that are woven on the surface of the material, because they don't split or pick up unnecessary threads. For your crewel embroidery, don't make a mistake and buy darners. They have big eyes, but are far too long and difficult to handle. (When stabbing in and out of your embroidery frame, your fingers can't hold a long needle close enough to the point to get proper control.) Remember that the needle you use should always be slightly thicker than the thread, to open up a passage for it to pass through easily. Without this, constant passing of the wool will wear it out.

Open Work

I always more or less assumed I could imitate the beautiful open-work embroidered designs my mother once worked (for my own christening dress, no less!) but I was wrong. Can you tell me how it's done?

First you must begin by outlining the shape you want with 2 lines of trailing worked side by side. To do trailing, take fine whipping stitches closely over a bundle of 3 or more loose threads, to form the effect of a smooth raised cord. In the diagram: come up at A, go over the threads and down at B, almost in the same hole as A. Repeat, placing each stitch very close side by side.

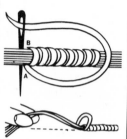

Now, cut away your fabric close against the trailing, inside the shape. Draw out the threads of the fabric inside the shape. Cut 2 threads and leave 2 threads in both directions, just inside the trailing, to give an over-all lattice effect. These threads are then whipped together to form a mesh into which other patterns can be woven, if desired. Remember, as always, to stretch your fabric tightly in a frame. When doing the trailing, pull the bundle of couching threads firmly in the direction you are working. This helps to make the line smooth and firm, like a cord. The double row of trailing makes a firm framework for the open-work filling stitches.

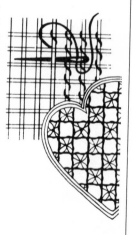

As for the kind of stitch you choose for the filling—you have a choice as wide as your inventiveness. The squared filling stitch, for example, comes in a number of variations, each with its distinctive feeling. What you must do to begin with, however, is to work on the lattice you created inside your design. With fine thread in a blunt needle, whip these threads together as shown in both directions. Having created this mesh, and reinforced it with the whipped thread, you can proceed and work over it with a squared filling stitch.

Pillows, Box

I think box pillows have a neat, formal look, but when I tried to make one for my finished design the result was anything but neat. Should I get it done professionally?

Don't consider yourself outclassed without another try. Start by making a margin, just as for the knife-edge pillow. Cut your strip for boxing (most are 1½ to 2 inches wide when finished, so after adding seam allowance cut a strip 2½ to 3 inches wide). The length should be the distance around the piece, plus a total of 1 inch for seam allowance, again. Baste cording or fringe to the right side of the needlework and the backing piece on the seam side. Lay the needlework piece on the boxing strip, right sides together (the boxing strip seam should be located at the middle of one of the sides of the needlework).

Stitch along on top of the basted cording stitches all the way around the piece, being sure to clip the boxing at the corners. Sew the 2 edges of the boxing together where they meet, using a ½-inch seam. Finally, place the backing piece on the boxing strip, right sides together (and facing the right side of the needlework). Stitch around the pillow, leaving a 6-inch opening. There you have it—a little more time-consuming than the knife edge, but really no more difficult.

The technique works for pillow designs of all sorts and all shapes—rectangles, triangles, circles, squares—even, with some ingenious adaptations, for those odd shapes that are all the rage now. So why not experiment with a parallelogram, or a trapezoid, or some mythical monster of your own devising? In most cases, when working with odd shapes, the important thing is to allow enough seam all around the edge. You'll probably be making lots of tiny snips into the turnbacks so your monster lies flat, fat and cozy.

Pillows, Knife Edge

I created a beautiful crewel design — *but please tell me how to make a* pillow!

We are certainly not going to let all that effort go to waste! You can do either a knife edge or a box. In the first, the front and back are sewn together, giving a knife edge; the second has a fabric strip forming a middle between front and back. For a knife-edge pillow (once the finished design is blocked), trim the un-worked fabric to a ½-inch margin all around; then cut whatever backing you want to the same size.

If you're adding piping or fringe, pin it to the right side of the needlework along the seam line, basting in place exactly along the edge of your stitching. It's even a good idea to overlap the stitching 1 or 2 threads, so no white canvas or background fabric shows around the edge of the finished pillow. Lay the needlework piece down on the backing, right sides facing each other. Baste together, starting at the center of each side, then stitch by machine through all thicknesses. Be sure to leave a ½-inch seam allowance and a 6-inch opening. Trim corners and excess margin and make tiny snips into the turn-backs at corners and curves.

Stuff the pillow with down, kapok or polyester. The "professionals" make a pillow form an inch bigger than your needlepoint pillowcase so that the finished pillow is nice and plump. To make a form, cut 2 pieces of muslin (always leaving ½ inch for seam), stitch all around, leave a 4-inch opening, turn right side out, and then fill this with whatever stuffing you choose. Close the opening with hand stitching, then stuff your pillow form into your pillowcase. You can fit your pil-lowcase with a 6-inch zipper, or hidden snaps, or even work decorative buttons or clasps as part of the overall design.

Pillows, Ribbon

What do I do with all the leftover ribbons now that my four daughters are grown up?

Rush out and get a pair of sharp scissors, tailor's chalk, ½ yard of muslin, ¼ yard of velvet—we're going to make a ribbon pillow! Machine- or hand-stitch the ribbons together, enough to give you a 10-inch strip that is 1½ yards long. Cut a paper pattern 6½ inches square and pin it on the ribbons (in diamond shape). Lay a ruler alongside and mark the diamond with the chalk. Mark 4 diamonds and then cut along the chalk lines. Join the squares so they create a center design, seaming them right sides together with ½-inch turnbacks. Finish off with eyelet edging.

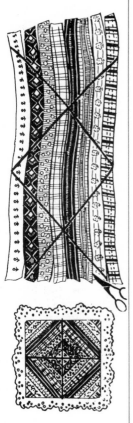

Now make a pillow form by making a pattern of your pillow, adding ½-inch seam allowance beyond your finished size. Following your pattern, cut out 2 shapes in muslin for back and front. Stitch it all around, leaving a ¼-inch opening. Turn it right side out, fill with polyester stuffing, and your inside pillow is ready. Now, cut out the back of your pillow from the velvet (or whatever fabric you prefer). Place your eyelet edging in position around the border of the ribbon square, with the raw edges of the eyelet facing away from the center of the pillow. Sew it in position (with ¼-inch lace in the seam), holding the ruffle toward the inside, right sides facing. Now pin the pillow to the front and to the ruffle. Stitch everything together, allowing ½ inch in the seam and leaving a 4-inch opening. Turn right side out and insert a pillow form. Close the opening with hand stitching. Now you can make another with the stitched ribbons left. Just join the leftover triangle pieces to make 4 squares, then begin again. You'll have enough to give each daughter her ribbons back in a useful and decorative object that would please any woman.

Plaidpoint Stitch

Did I hear correctly? Is there really a "plaid-point" stitch? Why go to such trouble reproducing a tartan on canvas when you can buy plaid fabrics?

For one thing, plaidpoint will wear 10 times longer than any fabric, which makes it perfect for rugs and pillows, and it's reversible, so there's no need for lining. And it's soft and light, so it's perfect for things like men's vests. And you can experiment with a whole rainbow of nontraditional colors. And . . . and . . . but follow these easy instructions, and you'll find out for yourself.

This stitch is reversible, so you must always use enough thread to complete 1 line. Run any thread joins invisibly into the previous stitches. To begin, make a slanting stitch across one intersection of the canvas; then, with the needle slanting as in the diagram, come up 1 thread below, and repeat to form a vertical line, skipping every other stitch. By slanting the needle as in the diagram, you will form an identical stitch on the reverse side. Be sure to work *all* the vertical lines right across the canvas first. By doing these complete rows you will be establishing your plaid pattern. For example, you begin by working 2 vertical rows of white, then 2 rows of red, 2 of white, 4 of red, 3 of green and so on, until the entire plaid is laid out.

Only when these vertical rows are completed should you start on the horizontals. When you repeat the pattern with the horizontal rows your reversible plaid turns out—as if by magic!—to be in fact reversible. You may be wondering why you can't start with all the horizontal rows. Well, the truth is you can, except that traditionally one sets up a loom by always working the vertical rows first, and there is something to be said for following traditional ways at times.

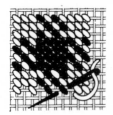

Point de Paris

I've managed to salvage some whole pieces from a lace bridal gown that must be more than a century old. I would like to use these pieces (which are still in very good condition) as part of a larger pillow design. What kind of stitching do you think would be most useful to hold the lace?

Your precious lace would look perfect if stitched to the background fabric with Point de Paris (or pin) stitch. The effect is a series of open-work holes, made by pulling the fabric tightly together with fine thread (1 strand of embroidery floss) and a large blunt needle, perhaps a tapestry No.18. Because you must pull tightly, this is one time when you should work in your hand, not a frame, wrapping the material firmly around your finger to hold it taut as you stitch. The holes made become dominant, and the connecting stitches are almost invisible. And because each stitch is taken twice, it's very strong.

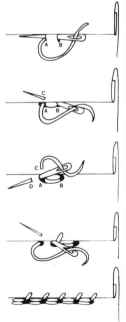

Follow the diagram: using a blunt tapestry needle, come up at A under the hem, go in at B and return again at A in the same hole. Now go in again at B and come up at C, directly above A in the hem. Return again to A, and come up at D.

Now repeat steps 1, 2 and 3, wrapping each stitch tightly to form large holes. In order to hold the holes firmly apart, each stitch must be wrapped twice; so it is best to first practice Point de Paris with heavier thread, working loosely, so that you can clearly see each stitch and master the repeated movements of the needle. You'll find the stitch works beautifully on either open-weave linen or on any fine material such as lawn, muslin, organdy or silk. Point de Paris is most suitable for hems and is very effective in shadow appliqué; it borders the appliqué shapes with a row of open-work holes.

Pompons

I'd love to finish off my beach hat—already decorated with crewel leaves and flowers—with pompons. How can I make them?

Cut 2 cardboard discs (shirt cardboard is just fine) with holes in the center; place them together and wrap with wool by rolling lengths into small enough balls to pass through the holes. When enough wrapping closes the hole, slip the point of your scissors between the discs and clip the wool all around the outer edge. Draw a strand of yarn between the discs, wrap it several times around and secure with a double knot. Leave the ends long for attaching the pompon to your bolero! You can now buy handy, reusable pompon "donuts" at notions stores.

Protecting Your Needlework

Should I line my crewel curtains and valances? If so, must I use real Irish linen?

Lining is a must because direct sunlight is destructive to crewel linen. Make an interlining too; "millium" is good, for it's thermal and keeps out heat, cold and sunlight. Expensive linen isn't necessary; a sheet will do.

I'd put up shades on the windows for extra protection. (Did you know that museums hang their priceless embroideries behind heavy velvet draperies?) And while we are on the subject, never use spotlights or overhead lighting — they are as destructive as direct sun. And when you store, never use plastic (the fabric can't "breathe") or tissue paper (there's acid in tissue). Use old, clean Turkish toweling or old fabric, and store on rollers. Remember — crewel and embroidery are among the most beautiful, but also most perishable, of the arts.

Quilting

I made several quilts, joining the blocks together by machine. A friend told me the ideal way is to join them by hand, so I can do them anywhere – train, plane or even a dinner party, where everyone could pitch in, like an old quilting bee. But she forgot to tell me what kind of stitch to use. Which stitch would you recommend?

The ideal stitch is the "blind" stitch because it is completely invisible. Slide the needle horizontally through the top of 1 square and hop over and slide the needle through the top of the other square, taking up just a small amount of fabric in each instance. Continue doing this with each of your squares, until the whole quilt is held together by this invisible network of thoroughly invisible straight stitches. You will find that having learned this stitch you have added a perfect means of joining any seam (on the right side) to your repertory.

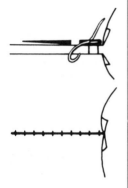

I've arrived at the critical moment when I must join my finished quilt, the filling and the background together. What is the best stitch for doing this?

I always like to recommend the simplest of stitches for such practical purposes. So stitch away with the basic broad basting stitch. As you can see from the illustration, it practically explains itself. Just make your vertical rows a few inches apart and remember to begin and end each line of stitching with a crisscross basting stitch. You go over the entire surface of the fabric until it is covered with broad rows of stitching. Because it is so firm, this stitch is ideal for holding layers of material together. When you are all finished, they will seem like one.

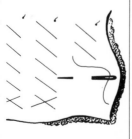

Quilting

I have been working on a quilt for what seems like ages—and I'm losing patience! How much can I leave unquilted and still get good wear and launderability?

If you use polyester for your batting, which most modern quilters do because it fluffs up beautifully when washed, you can leave a space up to about 6 inches unquilted, and the piece will wear and wash without the batting separating. If you're using cotton batting, you'll have to quilt much closer together, with the rows of stitches no more than 2 inches apart. Polyester is available in sheets (for quilting) and in fibrous bulk for pillow making and other stitchery projects. It's easy to work with and is completely washable.

I'm going to do a "wedding ring" design quilt for my parents' golden wedding anniversary— but how much quilting thread will I need?

If your quilt is double-bed size, you'll need between 2 and 3 spools (that's if you stick to the traditional 8 stitches to the inch). A single bed needs 1 spool, and queen, a full 3.

The quilt I recently made is lovely, but I can't use it half the year because it's much too warm for comfort. Is there such a thing as a "cool" quilt?

With the great popularity of quilts (I hope you've had a chance to see some of the museum collections), there have been all sorts of experiments, and "summer" quilts is one of them. Proceed with your quilt top as you would ordinarily, but instead of filling it with polyester batting, get some lightweight flannel at a fabric shop, or use a double thickness of bed sheeting.

Quilts and Quilting

Quilting is such the rage today that I must try one. Can I start from scratch?

Why not start small — not a whole, bed-size quilt, but with a "crazy" pillow. "Crazy" does not describe a mental state but the jumble of odd-shaped patches sewn together haphazardly. Gather some scraps of cotton print and begin to sew them, slightly overlapping, onto a square of muslin that has been stretched taut in a frame. Hold the pieces together with the feather stitch, a beautiful old crazy-quilt stitch that is actually easier than the traditional quilting stitch.

I just began to assemble the 60 pieces I've cut for my "Grandmother's Flower Garden" quilt – and they don't line up! What's wrong?

The same thing I've done myself — not cut the squares exactly even. Cutting (whether your design calls for squares, triangles, hexagons, etc.) is the most important step. You need sharp scissors, a sharp pencil and some sheets of fine sandpaper. Yes, sandpaper! Transfer your design onto the sandpaper first. Then when you sketch the design onto your base fabric, the sandpaper template, placed face down, will grip the material and assure precision. (Use an old pair of scissors to cut the sandpaper, of course.) Keep in mind these points when cutting: press your fabric nicely before you cut it into shape, and leave a ¼-inch seam allowance on every piece. If, however, you're working your quilted pieces by machine and not hand-stitching them, you don't have to press each individual piece. Wait until you join 2 pieces together, then press them. And, one more hint, if you press the seams to one side, rather than flattening them open, they'll be much stronger.

Quiltpoint

I love the "look" of patchwork quilts. How can I re-create that look in needlepoint?

Just by using your imagination, and some simple stitches! Combine quilting and needlepoint and we have "quiltpoint," an intriguing way to translate the homespun look and sumptuous feel of a quilt into any kind of needlepoint project for rugs, wall hangings, wingback chairs, etc. Quiltpoint also makes a wonderful background for a regular needlepoint design because it has the squared effect of patchwork as well as a "puffy" look, as if you've been quilting and quilting for hours. What could be a simpler stitch, as you can see from the diagram. Once you have the first rows counted, the rest goes like magic.

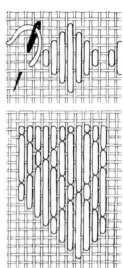

Finished effect

Repairs

The crewel dining room chair covers I slaved over are beginning to show their age at the edges. Can I do anything about it?

I think the best thing to do is to take the covers off and iron a layer of fine lawn to the back of them with Stitch Witchery or Wonderunder—that fusible adhesive material that's available everywhere these days. With very sharp scissors, cut your background fabric away close around the embroidery so that no material shows around the edge (it won't fray, because the adhesive makes the embroidery stick to the lawn). Then mount a piece of new material in a frame, pin and baste your design to it, and stitch it all around the edge with invisible stitches. Always bring your needle up into the background material first and go *down* into the embroidery, since the needle poking up from below might disturb it!

Repairs and Restorations

I hesitate to touch my great-great-grand-mother's sampler without your advice. It's dated 1868, so there's no wonder the threads are breaking apart. What can I do to save it?

Let me tell you a method museums use to restore and repair their old embroideries. Take a piece of muslin or fine linen and stretch it in an embroidery frame. Lay the sampler on top, without putting it in the frame. Baste the work down and hold it firm with tiny stitches in cotton floss, which will sink invisibly between your embroidery and the fabric. Then, using a single thread of cotton floss and a very fine needle (No. 9 or 10 crewel has a long eye and is very easy to thread), hold the design to the back and take tiny running stitches (in rows if the fabric is in really bad condition). Museums take one more step when a piece is in really bad condition—they cover the surface with fine net or tulle in matching color.

In our church basement we discovered some altar hangings that must be over 100 years old. Can they be salvaged, even though all the silk around the embroidery has rotted away?

It's certainly worth the effort! Put some linen in an embroidery frame — a piece large enough to cover the entire hanging. Take the embroidery and lay it over the linen. Baste it and then cut away the old silk, little by little, sewing down the embroidery as you go so that the design retains its original shape. You can use clear nylon thread for sewing and your stitches will be completely invisible. Linen is a good, strong material for this background and will give the hangings years of new life. More power to all you repairers, restorers and preservers!

Rice Stitch

I worked a small area rug in cross stitch and found it did not wear well. Is there a more durable and practical stitch?

Since you've obviously mastered the simple cross stitch, move up to the rice stitch, a marvelously hard-wearing geometric stitch that is ideal for things that must take a lot of wear. Make a cross stitch from A to B and C to D over 6 threads of the canvas. Then cross each of the 4 arms of the cross stitch with slanting stitches. Come up at E, midway between B and D, go in at F, midway between D and A (E and F are each 3 threads away from D). Next come up at G, halfway between B and C, and go back to E. Come up at H halfway between C and A. Continue the pattern by going in at F and up at G. Complete the pattern by going in at H. The needle is shown coming up at J to begin another pattern.

Rickrack

I've discovered, at the bottom of my work basket, yards and yards of rickrack (you know, that zigzag piping). What can I do to make good use of it?

You seem to be no more a fan of rickrack than I. It always looked so machine-made to me, but once I hit on the idea of combining it with handmade stitches, I became a convert. How about stitching rows of the rickrack above the hem of an evening skirt, then doing the tied herringbone stitch between the rows. First work a line of plain herringbone; with a blunt needle and contrasting thread, slide the needle under the cross, pointing the needle toward the center of the line. Twist thread over and under the needle. Draw tight to knot it and continue to work a knot on each cross.

Roumanian Stitch

I followed instructions carefully, but my Roumanian stitches pulled away from each other, and the material shows. Now what?

Well, let's take it step by step, and look for the danger spots. First, come up at A, down at B, up at C, down and over at D. If this small stitch maintains its slant well, the stitches will fit closely, with no separation. Now, for the next row, come up at E, below but touching A, go down at F, below but not touching B; leave a loop. Then come up at G, close to and immediately below C, inside the loop; draw tight. Now, go down over thread at H, directly below D, exactly as above. Carefully avoid going into the exact same holes as the stitch above, because that is sure to pull your stitches apart.

In an old needlework book there's an illustration for a stitch that looks exactly like the Roumanian, but it's called the "New England Economy Stitch." Are they the same?

Yes, and the reason why is typically "New England." Those thrifty needleworkers knew that the Roumanian stitch is a great yarn saver, because it leaves practically no wool on the back of the embroidery. So they embraced their Balkan cousin and renamed the stitch. And we can understand why the stitch was so popular. Back in those days, embroidery wasn't as simple as dashing down to the local shop and picking up a shopping bag full of yarn. They had to start from scratch, with a sheep, cleaning, spinning and dyeing. No wonder at all that they were delighted with an embroidery stitch that left nothing but 2 little stitches of wool on the back. With today's cost of materials, you may be inspired to try the Roumanian stitch!

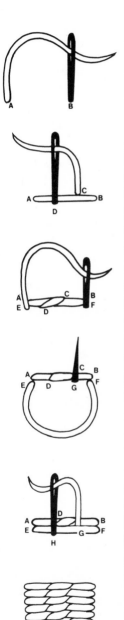

73

Rugs

I'm tempted to begin a needlepoint rug, but I've never tried anything so ambitious before. How do I begin?

I'm a firm believer in projects that really show off your work — and what better way than in a beautiful rug! You'll need a double-thread canvas, with firm, interlocked weave, and a mesh size of from 5 to 10 threads to an inch. Either Penelope or mono canvas can be used, and each has certain advantages. With Penelope you can combine petitpoint and grospoint in the same design, because the weave of the canvas is designed to allow this. Because of the firmness of the double threads, Penelope canvas can be made in larger sizes of mesh than mono. With mono canvas, geometric stitching is easier, since single threads give you more freedom to do a variety of textured stitches.

You'll have no trouble finding wool for your rug, because rug wool comes in several weights and lovely colors. But you may also use as many strands of Persian wool as your canvas needs; it's also very hard wearing.

Now for the stitch. Working on Penelope you can use the half cross stitch, as it will be so much more economical with wool, and the Penelope canvas is firmly woven with its double strands, so everything will stay neatly in place. Cross stitch is another stitch which works well with Penelope canvas. Like the rice stitch, it is extremely hard wearing and most suitable for rugs. Of course, you must remember that a cross stitch will take twice as long to do, because your needle must revisit every stitch you put down, going over it to make the cross. But it wears twice as long.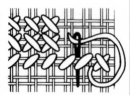

Don't let the sheer size of a rug inhibit you — reduce it all to squares that you can manage in a frame and join them together one by one as they are completed.

It isn't "simple" at all! Why do I keep fumbling with my latch hook?

All right, pick up your hook and follow me! Hold the hook in one hand and in the other, hold a strand of yarn. Fold the yarn over the shaft of the hook, making sure that the ends of the yarn are even. The hook latch is open, remember. Hold onto the yarn as you insert the head of the hook under the canvas thread and up into the hole immediately above. Then push the hook forward until the entire latch passes under the thread. Now, as you pull the hook back toward you, the latch will open, allowing you to lay the 2 ends of the yarn between the latch and the hook. Draw the hook toward you and the latch will close around both ends of the yarn. Release the yarn. Continue to pull the latch through the canvas.

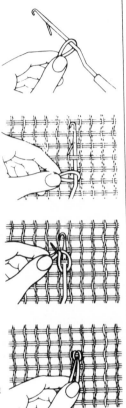

What happens now is the secret: the cut ends of the yarn are pulled through the loop, forming a knot. All you have to do is give a gentle tug to the ends to secure them. Always work with the knotted part toward you, so that knots are all tied in the same direction. If your "pull" is even, you won't have too much snipping of loose ends.

What would be the best kind of canvas on which to do a latch hook rug?

I guess you mean what size canvas to select, since the quality of most canvas is standard. The principle is basically the same as in other kinds of needlework — the size of the mesh of the canvas indicates the number of threads per inch. In rug work, however, that number indicates how many knots — not stitches — are required to cover a given area. Penelope weave canvas is most often used for latch hook rugs; No. 4 Penelope will give a thick, tight pile. You may use 3½ or even 5 for your rug, although you'll have to work with a lighter-weight yarn with No. 5.

Rugs

I thought all those "shaggy" rugs were the same thing and made the same way. But now I gather there are different kinds. What's the difference?

The "shaggy" look rug you've probably seen in department stores was most likely a Rya — that is, if it was worked on a heavy foundation fabric. The Rya pile is made by working yarn in a series of knots on this base fabric. A needle is used to pierce the fabric, then the knot (called the Ghiordes) is tied. Long loops are left between knots; as each row is completed the loops are cut, creating the loose, slightly uneven pile.

Rya rugs are an ancient Scandinavian art, going back at least to the tenth century. Latched rugs, on the other hand, are done on a canvas (most often Penelope). The yarn is precut and of uniform size, traditionally 2½ inches long. The yarn is worked into the canvas and actually knotted in place by the latch, a simple tool with a blunt hook on the end (for slipping between the canvas mesh and grasping the looped yarn). The "latch" is directly under the hook and opens to catch the yarn, hold it fast, then pull it through the canvas, knotting it securely — and permanently! — in place.

One of the dividends of a latch hook rug is that two can work on it at the same time — not from either end of the rug, however. You and your partner both work on the same row, one from the center to the right edge, the other from the left edge to the center. That much "togetherness" should guarantee that your knots and pulls will be even, but if you notice some different lengths of yarn when the rug is finished, just snip them all even with a sharp scissors as if you were a barber. I've known of several marriages that were saved working together this way!

Samplers

I have nothing against books – and certainly not against yours! But I hate to stop my embroidery to riffle through one looking for the right stitch. What's a convenient way of keeping stitches at hand?

Why not make your next project a dictionary-sampler, where you collect small samples of all the various kinds of stitches you might have to call on at a moment's notice? With each stitch worked, you'll have an instant preview of how it will look in your design. For example, one "page" of your dictionary can be devoted to all the kinds of stem stitches, another to the satin stitches, another to chain stitches, cross, back, weaving and filling. Contrasting colors will help you keep things handy for easy reference.

Satin Stitch

I guess I read only half the directions – the part that said satin stitches are just so many threads laid side by side. And that's how my crewel leaves look – just so many threads.

Practice, practice! That's the only way to get those satin stitches meticulously even. The directions you forgot say: First outline with split stitch. Start in the center (to be certain of the exact angle); work slanting stitches close together across the shape, coming up and going down outside the split stitch. Work up to the tip, then start at center again and finish working shape to the bottom. Do not pull too tightly. Here's another trick: to maintain the slant, come up close at the upper edge and go down with a slight space between the stitches on the lower edge. Working your stitches this way tends to exaggerate the slant of each stitch without flattening it.

Satin Stitch

You said don't do it, but I did it — worked more than ½ inch satin stitch on my crewel pocketbook cover! Can I rescue the snagged stitches before they all go?

There are some people — mostly my own children, I sometimes think — who have to "do" every "don't" at least once, just to test it. Well, think positively and turn your mistake into a new design plus. Tie down your loose satin stitches with a back stitch, as illustrated here. More than 1 row of back stitches may be worked, if the area needs it. Don't pull the back stitch too tight, for that will spoil the evenness of the satin stitch underneath. Work the back stitch through the center of each shape, using the upper edge as a guideline. Needle comes up at A, and down at B, right into the hole made by the last stitch.

Scissors

What kind of scissors are best to use when doing needlework?

Actually, you'll need two kinds: a large, heavy-duty type for cutting canvas and skeins of yarn; and a small, sharp-pointed pair for cutting out mistakes and for cutting tails of your yarn as you work.

I'm a male needleworker, and proud of it — except for the dainty scissors my wife lets me use. Where do I find man-size scissors?

You could contact a surgical supply house and get something fitted for you — the points are wonderfully sharp, of course, and the proportion and balance would be perfectly suited to your particular needs.

Scottish Stitch

Is the plaid stitch I've heard you talk about the same as the Scottish stitch?

The Scots are very generous, so they've given us two stitches. Scottish stitch is a variation of flat stitch, which looks like a plaid. First you work a network of tent stitch squares, 5 stitches to each. Then fill in the squares with diagonal flat stitches. Your tent stitches should all slant in the same direction, but you could vary the slant of the flat stitches from row to row for an interesting effect. And while you're experimenting with the possibilities of the basic flat stitch (stitches worked diagonally over 1, 2, 3, 4, 3, 2, and finally 1 thread) you might also try alternating the squares with blocks of tent stitch. Here again, you could work the squares so that each block slants in the opposite direction.

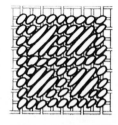

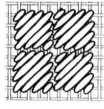

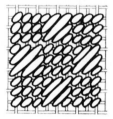

Scrim Embroidery

I just bought an authentic Roumanian blouse pattern which calls for "scrim" embroidery to be used in applying the decorations. Can you tell me what this is?

"Scrim" actually refers to a coarse-weave muslin fabric slightly stiffened and of sufficiently even weave to baste on top of a sheer fabric such as organdy. You then use the weave for counting out geometric cross-stitch borders. You work through the 2 layers of fabric, then ravel away the scrim — and no one will know how you worked so evenly without any apparent guidelines. Of course, the Stitch Witchery I often speak about can do the same thing. This gauzelike fabric is used the same way, and once you're done you just tear it away. All that can be seen is your perfectly designed embroidery!

Seeding

I've been working out a crewel embroidery design – some traditional stems and leaves. Somehow the outlined leaves seem dull and lifeless. What have I done wrong?

Details, details! God is all in the details, as the old adage has it. Your embroidery needs the zest that can come from one of the simplest of the so-called "filling" stitches. Try sprinkling the leaf patterns with simple seeding, either scattered evenly, each stitch slanting in a different direction, or massed closely to form a shaded effect. The stitch is simplicity itself: come up at A, go down at B a small distance away. Pull through, lightly. Come up at C, go down at D, across the first stitch, diagonally. Pull through so that the stitch forms a firm, round, slightly raised "bump" on the fabric — the perfect three-dimensional, tactile effect you want. When you work in a color that matches your background fabric, it has a particularly nice textured look — almost like Persian lamb fur!

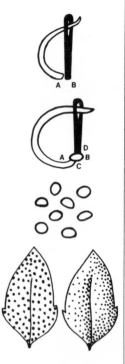

Sequins

I want to border the appliqué on my bolero vest with sequins. I was told I must coat my thread with beeswax first. Why?

The wax will protect the thread from the sharp edge of the sequins. This way there will be no fraying either while you are working or once you've finished. Beeswax couldn't be simpler to use, and you can find it at any notions department. Just thread the needle and draw the thread 2 or 3 times through the beeswax. The wax stiffens the thread, too, making it easier to handle. Candlewax is sometimes used for the same purpose, but it is not as "clingy" as beeswax.

Shadow Work

I have just seen the most magnificent organdy tablecloth in a neighborhood shop. It's worked in something called shadow stitch. I can't afford to buy one; can I make my own?

You certainly can, and at the same time introduce yourself to the delights of working on sheer fabric. When worked on organdy (or other sheer or opaque fabrics), certain stitches give you a clear silhouette that stands out beautifully against the transparent background.

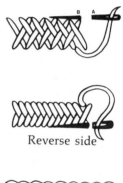

Reverse side

Shadow stitch (actually, a row of close herringbone stitches worked on the reverse side) is one of the best of these stitches. To begin, work a row of herringbone stitches (on the reverse side of the design area). Take 1 stitch from right to left, A to B on the diagram, on the lower outline of the design, and repeat it at the upper edge, going right into the same hole formed by the previous stitch. The effect is best if the stitches are taken very close together, as shown in this illustration of the reverse side.

When worked on organdy, the effect on the right side is an opaque band bordered by a row of back stitches, above and below. The closer the stitches, the more opaque and distinct this band will be — depending on how closely the stitches are worked. When areas are wide, do not work a wide band of stitching from one side to the other, as that would leave loose loops on the reverse side. Instead, break up the area into bands and work several rows of shadow stitch side by side to fill in the shape. Buy the sheerest organdy you can find, so your white thread will be a sharp contrast, white as sunshine and shadows on the snow — as romantic an effect as its name. This kind of work is, obviously, not for the timid needleworker, but if you are daring, you'll have a piece to treasure.

Shisha

I've seen the most fantastic mirror decorations on fabrics and pillows in a boutique — and now I want to copy that mirror technique onto a pair of bluejeans. What kind of stitch holds those little mirrors into place?

What you've been admiring is called shisha-work (*shisha* is the Indian word for mirror). It would be magnificent worked on new or old bluejeans!

You can buy small pieces of glass (glitters) at a notions store, or use sheets of aluminum foil backed with linen or cotton (Mylar). First place your mirror circle in position and hold in place with 2 small stitches. Come up at A and go down at B to make the horizontal stitch ⅓ down from the top of the circle. Come up at C. Continue around circle, from C to D, E to F, G to H, making a square. Repeat around circle, making 4 more stitches from I to J, K to L, M to N, O to P, to make a diamond on top of the square.

Now, using a blunt needle, come up at A in diagram 4. Slide needle under the holding thread and draw tight with the thread under the needle. Then take a small stitch into the fabric, close to the edge of the circle, from C to D. With thread looped under needle as shown in diagram 5, draw tight. Repeat step as shown in diagram 4, sliding needle under the holding threads, and draw tight with the thread under the needle. Repeat step in diagram 5, but go down under the same hole INSIDE the loop at O. Come up at F with thread under needle. Continue, repeating steps 6 and 7, to make a close band of stitching around the circle. As you can see, you have to carefully catch all the holding stitches to conceal them.

For a final note, if you can't find Mylar and are afraid of glass, try cutting tiny circles out of a postcard and covering them with foil.

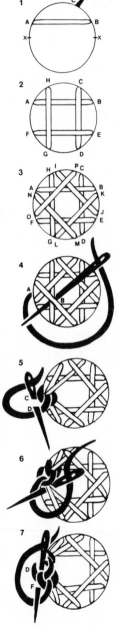

Silk

Maybe it's the name and all the exotic associations, but I just automatically think that working in silk is different from the other kinds of needlework. Can you tell me something about silk embroidery?

Exotic, yes, but it's not altogether different. One of the main things that sets embroidery done in silk apart from the others is, of course, the finer scale and smoother texture you can achieve. But silk threads can be used in exactly the same way as crewel and needlepoint wools. And any of the stitches used in crewel embroidery can be worked in silk.

Real silk threads may be hard to find, although they are available in various forms, both as floss or twisted like a fine cord (Pearsall's Filo Floss and Filoselle Silk). If the expense and the difficulty of finding real silk stops you, why not experiment with cotton instead? Although cotton is not as soft or as rich-looking as silk, it does have certain advantages. For one, the mercerized embroidery floss and the kinds of crochet cotton available come in a good range of colors, wear better and are washable.

Gold used to be the constant companion of silk, but that tradition has gone the way of so many others. So your silken (even if cotton!) stitches can liven up an old pair of bluejeans with a few delicate daisies, as well as create marvelous scrolls around a seed pearl on your evening bag. Just remember that if you work with fine silk on a rather stretchy open-weave linen, you must back the linen with another material (a lightweight linen or muslin), to make it firm. Just baste the two together, embroider the design right through, then cut away the backing around the stitches on the wrong side. And once you get to be an expert at working with silk, you can go on to doing gold and black work!

Smocking

When I was a little girl — and I won't say when — it seems I was always dressed in a dress that had lots of smocking on its front. I never was taught how to do this kind of needlework — but now my grandchildren are asking me to show them. Can you help me?

Smocking is coming back, and not just because it's beautifully decorative. Smocking really began as a very practical method of giving elasticity to a garment, allowing a blouse or workshirt to "give" with the wearer's movement — whether a child at play or a man swinging an ax. Smocking is based on gathering material across the front and back of the blouse, forming very regular rows of exactly the same length. The gathers or folds should be drawn up closely, not more than ½ inch apart, and the stitches should be of equal length on both sides of the material. When the gathers are done, the embroidery is worked from fold to fold.

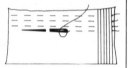

In gathering you must use very strong thread, securing the starting end well. The line of gathering stitches must be true, vertically and horizontally. The most traditional smocking stitch is simple stem stitch (called the outline or rope stitch in smocking). Working across, you take 1 stitch into each fold, either in single, double or triple, holding the thread on the same side of the needle at all times. You can also do a cable stitch by holding the thread alternately above or below the needle, which gives a broader line. Either of these stitches makes a firm edge at the top or bottom of a band of smocking. The trellis stitch is really just a further development of stem. Simply descend for 5 stitches with the thread *above* the needle, and then ascend for 5 stitches with the thread *below*. When working the trellis, always keep the needle at a right angle to the fold.

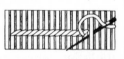

There is a woman in our club who can do the most elaborate smocking patterns just by her eye. She actually gathers the threads without any kind of guidelines or patterns! I tried to imitate her, but I soon wound up with a mess, of course. Is there a way I can learn to smock, neatly?

There's help on the way! Go out and buy some checked gingham — you'll love the finished results. Buy 3 times the width of your finished smocked panel. Begin by threading the needle with enough strong thread to complete a horizontal line of running stitches (you can't join in the middle if you run out), and secure it firmly at the beginning with a knot and a back stitch. Then make a horizontal row of running stitches, going in at one side of a square, out at the other. Repeat these steps exactly underneath, 1 row below, and continue to the depth that you want your smocking to occupy.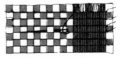

Now comes the exciting part! When you gather it all up you will find (provided, of course, that you have made no mistakes) that your folds all gather up in only 1 color. For instance, if you picked up only the blue squares, the folds will be only blue; if you picked up all the white squares, you will have all white folds. Now you must secure the gathering threads — but only for the time being. Do this by twisting the threads around pins to hold the gathers in place while you are smocking. Work your stitches, then remove the gathering threads and your stitching — blue on the white or white on the blue — will look beautiful.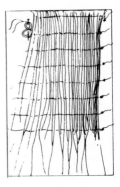

But, I hear you say, what if I want to smock plain fabric? Transfer patterns! These, with evenly spaced dots, are beginning to be available at most specialty needlework stores. Transfer them accurately with a hot iron. Then go in at one spot, up at the next and go gathering on your merry way!

Split Stitch

I began what I thought would be lovely rose leaves in a slanting satin stitch. But there's nothing lovely about the ragged edges. How can I get my stitches even?

I hate to ask it, but did you remember to outline your design first in the *split* stitch? No building is stronger than its foundation, and you've just found out that no satin-stitch leaf is neater than the split-stitch padding that gives it a crisp outline. And don't think you're throwing away effort on a stitch that will later be covered over by another stitch. Follow the diagram: the needle comes up at A, goes down at B. Next the needle comes up at C, piercing through the center of the stitch, from below, splitting it exactly in the middle. Then the needle goes down at D, the same distance away from C as B is from A. To go around curves, shorten your stitches slightly.

Stem Stitch

I can do it, but I can't seem to get it to look like a natural outline in my design — how do I master the simple stem stitch?

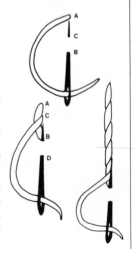

Here are a few hints. When working an outline, hold the thread away from the shape and toward the outside of curves. This will make the outline roll outward instead of falling inward and becoming "spiky." You can see in the diagram that C is halfway between A and B; in step 2, the needle enters the same hole made by the thread going in at B. Thread may be held to left or right, but it remains on the same side for the whole line. If your stitch is correct, you will have a line of back stitch on the reverse side, with each stitch fitting into the holes of the previous ones.

Stitching Technique

Is there a "correct" way to begin and end my stitches when doing needlework?

In beginning needlepoint, place a knot in 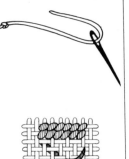 your thread, go through to the back of the canvas and start about ½ to 1 inch away. The thread lying at the back will be locked in by the stitches that follow, and you can cut the knot off. When ending, bring the thread to the front about 1 inch from where you are working, leaving the end hanging there until the thread on the back is covered. Then, cut off the thread on the front close to the canvas. You are, of course, working in a frame or hoop, and it's most unprofessional to be seen peering under it — for anything! When doing embroidery work, take 2 tiny, invisible stitches in the design line on the wrong side, which isn't important when doing crewel work, since it will be backed. End off with 2 small back stitches on an outline or inside the shape of a design which will later be covered.

I've always been a "tight" knitter. How do I know if my needlework tension is correct?

Always pull your yarn smoothly and consistently, not so loose that the stitches look lumpy and not so tight that they pull the canvas. Even tension comes from practice!

Why do the strands of my wool get thinner as I work my needlepoint canvas?

The friction of the canvas is thinning the yarn as you pull it through the holes. You may be using a longer thread than you should. I find that an 11- or 12-inch length of wool is perfect, for just about the time it's starting to thin, you're ready to end off.

Stump Work

At a needlework "show and tell" meeting, we were shown a fascinating piece of work with raised stitches in high relief. The owner casually said it was stump work. Now I'm dying to know how she did it.

Stump work must have been the first way any needlework decided to "stand up and be counted"! You too can get those super-textured stitches by working flat crewel in high relief. Combine these raised stitches with some of the normally raised ones (padded satin, French knots on stalks, Turkey work), or with flat crewel stitches for an interesting effect. For instance, fur for animals or a flower petal can be worked in stem stitch left in loose loops so that each stitch is raised. If you're a bit timid about trying it, you might begin with a raised frame worked all around some flat crewel embroidery.

Let me show you the buttonhole on a raised band. First lay a series of parallel stitches close together as in step 1. Lay a second row of stitches over the first, keeping the stitches away from the edges (step 2). Several decreasing rows may be worked in this way to create a raised center. Now lay a series of parallel stitches across the band just under ¼ inch apart. Using a blunt needle, come up at A, form a loop with the thread and, without going through the material, slide under the first bar from B to C. Draw down toward you until the thread is snug. Now you have a buttonhole stitch on the horizontal bar. Now repeat step 4, sliding the needle under the thread from D to E and work to the base of the bar this way. When you have reached the base of each line, anchor the final stitch by going down through the material over the button-hole loop at F, as shown in step 6. Now you can experiment with other stitches to create your own variation of stump work.

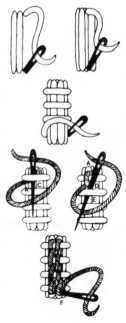

At a museum I saw incredibly beautiful raised needlework that the guide called "stump work." Is there a project I can do?

Yes, you can create your own stump work project, and have an unusual, "3-D" embroidery just like the kind that was the rage in the seventeenth century. You could cover a pillbox or a jewelry case, or you could frame a mirror, or just work a piece and set it under a glass-top coffee table. Since the secret is all in the raised fabric, you'll first need muslin for lining the padded area. For the padding you can use regular cotton, or polyester wadding or even the lamb's wool sold for protecting corns! Because the stitches are to be raised, you should work on a square frame or hoop large enough to enclose the entire design (a smaller hoop would press on and crush the padded stitches).

Traditional stump work was done on white satin, but you can use any fabric. Hands and faces of figures were raised with wooden molds and all kinds of lacy stitches (hollie point and trellis, for example) were raised by padding, then combined with flat stitches such as long and short and laid. You can apply any material to the background, cutting out the shape to be applied a little larger than the design, then fill the "bubble" that forms in the center with stuffing. Leave enough of the edge unstitched so you can push a padding between the layers of fabric. You sew your stitches over, not through, the padded surface. Use weaving, buttonhole or trellis (surface stitches) for this.

You could also embroider a variety of stitches on a separate piece of material, then appliqué and pad it. Turn back the edges of these stitched pieces and either sew them down like patches or just tack them here and there. All kinds of imaginative stump work can be done by applying needlepoint canvas shapes to a crewel background.

Tapestry

I've seen museum exhibitions of medieval tapestries, and I know that the art of this kind of needlework is more time-consuming than I am willing to give. But is there any way I could create the "feel" of one of these gems?

Yes, and it won't take you centuries! All you need are a No. 12 mesh canvas, 2-thread Persian wool, and your design. To get that tapestry-like weave on canvas, you use the long and short stitch, which is perfect. These long, even stitches give the vibrantly shaded effect of real tapestry, with strong vertical lines. The holes of your canvas force the threads to stay in place, which isn't always easy when you are doing the long and short stitch on linen. Remember to work the stitches of your design straight up and down, using the plain satin stitch when there is no room for color blending.

Sometimes you will need a clearcut outline, so use a fine outline stitch such as stem stitch or back stitch after the whole area has been filled in. The lustrous tapestry effect is achieved not only by the long stitches, but also by the rigidity of their direction. Certain wide areas may be all in one color, so an ideal stitch here is random bargello (actually long and short worked vertically, but in irregular lengths over the whole area). Tapestries lend themselves to strong color contrasts and to simple, clearcut and stylized shapes, so don't try to use too many shades of color and busy shapes. The dramatic effect of interlocking colors, with different shades softly blended in vertical lines, will give your tapestry the beautiful look you so admired in those museum pieces — and you'll be amazed at how quickly it's done. Don't limit yourself to traditional subjects — almost any design will work with this technique—and you'll soon have your own "exhibition" piece!

Tassels

How can I make my own tassels to give a finishing touch to my needlepoint pillow?

Cut a piece of cardboard the length of the tassel, then wrap yarn around it — a lot for fat tassels, a little for thin ones. Thread some yarn through the top of the twists, knot it to hold the yarn together and then slide the yarn off and bind it tightly with another piece of yarn about ⅔ of the way up to form the knob. Trim the bottom evenly and use the ends you left hanging from the upper knot to sew the tassel firmly to the pillow. I suggest you test to see if your pillow really needs the tassels first by holding up a bunch of yarn.

Tent Stitch

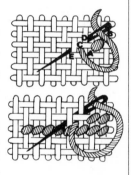

I am really confused about names — is the needlepoint tent stitch the same as the continental and the basket weave?

"Continental" really means a tent stitch worked in horizontal and vertical lines. A basket weave is also a tent stitch, but one that is worked diagonally, while grospoint, demipoint and petitpoint are just names to describe large, medium and small tent stitches on canvas.

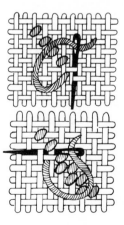

To do the basic horizontal tent, come up at A, go down at B (1 thread above and 1 to the right of A). Come up at C, 1 thread to the left, and level with A. Repeat, going in at D, up at E, making a horizontal row, working from right to left. Then turn the canvas and work a second row above the first, bringing up the needle in the same holes.

Tent stitch may also be worked in diagonal lines. When working from top to bottom, the needle is placed vertically; when working from bottom to top, the needle is horizontal.

Theorems

I was digging through an antique shop in the country and I came upon a beautiful painting on velvet. The old shopkeeper told me it was a "theorem," and he would sell it to me if I knew how to solve it. What is it?

When I went to the library to read up on "theorems," the librarian brought me stacks of books on geometry! But now I know that theorems are paintings of flowers and fruits, usually stenciled — and hence called theorems because of the precise, exacting method of transferring and painting the layers of stencils onto cloth. Today you can translate this old art into a fascinating needlework project.

First, sketch your design on a very flat matte velvet, on a small scale so you can decide on the colors. Then enlarge the design to the size you wish on white paper, and tape it to the back of your velvet, which should be stretched taut in an artist's stretcher frame. Then take a gooseneck lamp and put it behind the stretcher frame, maneuvering the light so that the clear silhouette of the design shines through the velvet. Trace the pattern with a fine-tipped permanent marker, changing the angle of the frame so that the light silhouettes each area of the design as you need it. This is what I call the "light box" method, which is perfect for velvet — transferring with carbon paper is impossible in this case.

When you stitch on velvet, use a chenille needle — it's short and has a nice big eye and makes a clear, open passage for the thread to pass through. Use the simplest stitches (satin or laid work), ones that give a bold, clear effect. To make distinct shapes in stitches, cut out the shapes in postcard-weight paper, lay these down on the velvet and then stitch right through them. When you remove the paper, you'll love the crisp edges to your stitches.

Thimbles

I'm not sure thimbles are necessary in needlework. What do you think?

Oh, definitely! And use one each on the middle finger of each hand when you embroider in a frame, pushing the needle back and forth. In quilting, you take little running stitches, sewing with one hand rather than pushing the needle back and forth. The "sewing" hand on top needs a metal thimble to push; the hand underneath guides the needle, so it needs protection from constant stabbing. A leather finger guard will protect you, will not blunt the needle, but will allow you to still feel the needle as it goes through the layers of fabric. So by all means, do as our mothers did and thimble your fingers!

Tramé

Would you please explain "tramé" to me? I was told that it was a kind of stitch used in needlepoint, but I've never seen it used.

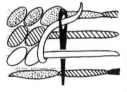

Tramé is not a stitch but an under-stitching, used to guide your needlepoint design. In tramé, long horizontal threads of wool are laid down in the exact color of the pattern. You then cover the lines of wool with the half cross stitch in the same colors. Tramé has become popular because you can see exactly what the design and coloring look like before you begin. And tramé is extremely hardwearing because of the threads lying underneath the stitches. Tramé kits are expensive because all those horizontal threads need to be laid down by hand. I know, because I once undertook to "tramé" six chair seats for a friend. It took almost as much time laying down the threads as working the design, but it wasn't nearly as satisfying.

Transferring Designs

I have the most beautiful design for some needlepoint pillows — but the design is on wallpaper! How do I get it on canvas?

Begin with acetate (that clear, glasslike paper you'll find in an art supply store), a permanent (nonrunning!) felt-tipped magic marker and masking tape. Tape the acetate over the area of the wallpaper you want to transfer and trace it onto the acetate with smooth, flowing lines, using the felt pen. Lay the acetate over a sheet of opaque drawing paper so that your black lines stand out and can be copied. Tape the needlepoint canvas on top. Make sure all corners square up and then trace the design onto the canvas, using the permanent pen. Now either fill the colors with oil paint or work directly on the outlined canvas with wool, following the colors of the wallpaper—or, create your own color scheme!

I've just begun working on an embroidery kit that was manufactured in Europe and I've discovered to my dismay that the beautiful design isn't painted on the canvas —it's done on a graph, on a separate piece of paper! How do I get the design onto the canvas?

The graph paper should have the design already counted out for you, so you can follow this as you transfer. Start in the middle of your canvas and count outward; for example, you'll need 3 stitches of green, 2 of blue, etc. Work in a frame because then you can check the alignment of your stitches by tracking your needle across the mesh to see if they line up. Checking as you go along is most important — one or two false steps and you may wind up with a lopsided rose, which, as everyone knows, is much worse than a second-hand rose!

Someone told me to use carbon paper to transfer a design.— and now I have black smudges all over it as well as me. What should I have done?

You should have bought a packet of dressmaker's carbon, which doesn't smudge. Assuming you have the right kind now, fold your material in half and then in half again and crease the folds so that they will show clearly. Then smooth the material flat on a table and hold it down evenly on all 4 sides with masking tape. Next, fold the design into 4 equal parts, open it and lay it down on top of the fabric. Now slide a sheet of the (dressmaker's) carbon, face downward, between the paper and material (use blue carbon for light materials; white for dark ones). Anchor the paper with some heavy books or paperweights, and trace around the outside very heavily with a pencil. Make sure you are really engraving the design by lifting a corner of the fabric and checking.

I've used one of those new transfer pencils to get my delicate crewel embroidery design transferred, but I can hardly see the lines!

You have discovered for yourself one of the drawbacks to what is really a good shortcut in transferring. The transfer pencil is apt to rub off and doesn't provide a very clear, definite line, so delicate designs are out. The pencil works best for large, bold designs. When you do use the pink transfer pencil, outline the design on tracing or layout paper, then turn it face downward onto the material and iron it just the way you would a commercial transfer, using a fairly warm iron. Don't panic if the transfer line seems to go into the fabric rather thickly — it will eventually wash out. Transfer pencils are often given the very important sounding name of "hectographs."

Transferring Designs

I want to do a cross-stitch phrase on the back of my boyfriend's workshirt. How do I transfer the design onto the denim?

Baste a piece of single-weave needlepoint canvas over the area where the pattern is going. Stretch the area to be worked on in an embroidery frame and cross stitch the pattern through both thicknesses. (You'll see that your stitches are even because the straight lines of the canvas keep them that way.) When the design is finished, unravel the threads of the canvas at the edges and pull them right out, one by one, like pieces of straw. If your fabric is washable, it may be easier to do if you soak the embroidery in cold water first to soften the sizing of the canvas.

Can you tell me how to iron on the iron-on transfer pattern I just bought?

Begin by using the test design that you should find on the transfer. Get your iron to a moderate heat, place it on the paper (which should be face down on the fabric) and hold for about the count of five. As you lift the tissue paper, the whole thing should lift off easily, because the wax will have melted, leaving a clear impression on the fabric. If it sticks, put the iron down again and hold it longer. If you have to tear the paper away, you may end up with only a faint impression that is hard to follow. I usually find I have to lightly scorch the paper to get it really clear — but don't scorch the fabric. Transfer inks vary a lot, so do test the ink first.

I just heard that a wonderful new method is coming on the market. Instead of ironing, you just rub over the design with a pencil and — presto! — it's transferred easily, as often as you want, and washes out without a trace.

Could you invent a method of transferring the design of an antique quilt to a new top?

Necessity, not I, shall invent this one — based on the idea of "recycling" those plastic bags your dry cleaning comes in. First lay your new top fabric on the floor; cover the whole area with a single layer of plastic bags. Smooth out the old quilt top on top of both the new fabric and the plastic. Pin it in place, but pins only in the design, please! Working on a small area at a time, cut around the appliquéd shapes, cutting away both plastic bag and old background fabric. Place a brown paper bag on top and iron. The heat of the iron will melt the plastic, your appliqué pieces will be fused to the new background, and any extra plastic around the edge will adhere to the brown paper bag, not the iron. Now all you have to do is stitch around the edges of your shape to hold it permanently to the background fabric. (The plastic bagging will evaporate once the top is cleaned.)

Will you explain your "light-box" method of transferring designs?

Gladly, and again! Stretch your fabric onto an artist's stretcher frame. Secure it with tacks or a power stapler. Then, with masking tape, hold your *boldly* traced design to the reverse side, close against the linen. Make sure the edges of the design run parallel to the lines you marked lightly with pencil on the back of the linen to define its borders. Arrange a goose-necked lamp behind the stretcher frame, maneuvering the light so that a clear silhouette of the design shines through the fabric. Trace the pattern with a fine-tipped permanent marker. Did you know that our grandparents used to do basically the same thing — against a window pane! Fortunately, you don't have to be a contortionist using the light box method.

Tufting

When I (jokingly, I think) complained about the number of stitches that lay between me and the end of my pieced quilt coverlet, a neighbor told me that "tufting" was an alternative to quilting. What's tufting?

Your prayers may be answered by tufting, a technique of holding the 3 layers of a coverlet (the pieced top, the middle batting and the back) together by pulling through and knotting yarn, thread or string at spaced intervals, without sewing a stitch.

Start by laying the 3 layers on the floor, first the lining, right side down, then the batting, then the pieced top, right side up. Baste all 3 together with the broad basting stitch (to keep the filling in place until the tufting is finished). Mark where the tufting will be done: at 2-inch intervals with down filling; 8 to 10 inches with quilting batting. Use a strong and colorful embroidery thread, yarn or string, one that ties well and holds a knot. Bring the knotted double thread through all 3 layers to the top of the coverlet. Leave an excess of 2 inches when you cut off your stringing material. Now tie an ordinary double knot. The "sewing" job is done! And when they see the results, no one will accuse you of just wanting to save time — tufting has a lovely old-fashioned and homey look.

Now you have one last task to complete — sewing the edges of your quilt. You'll soon find that this is easier to do last, rather than making a "bag" and putting yarn filling into it later. If you do that you'll find that it's much harder to get the filling evenly distributed. You can finish the edges with binding or, if you prefer a plain edge, blind stitch them all around. Quilting is such a marvelous, to say nothing of historic, art that anything that helps us create quilts is welcome. And there's nothing anti-historic about shortcuts.

Tulle

I've just taken out my tulle bridal veil —and after 10 happy years I'd love to see it displayed. Can I embroider on tulle?

Yes, and beautifully! You simply darn with the same color thread as the net (usually white) and work back and forth through the tiny squares to form a pattern. Mark out your design with a permanent felt-tipped pen on some plastic-coated shelf paper. Baste your net to the paper and weave the outlines and patterns, following the lines. Use a blunt needle that will slide over the plastic and outline the shapes with a running stitch before filling them with geometric patterns. Vary the thickness of your thread for bold or lacy effects. (Your tulle may be too finely woven for darning; check on a corner with varying thicknesses of 6-strand embroidery thread.)

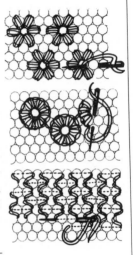

Twill Stitch

I've finished the central design, but I have a real chore filling in my needlepoint background. Can you suggest something interesting with a decided texture?

Try a background effect of twill-weave linen — in reality a simple large and small cross stitch, with a little horizontal stitch to create the appearance of twill. Begin by bringing the needle up at A (at the upper left corner). Count 6 threads down and 2 to the right and go down at B. Count 2 threads to the left, level with B and come up at C. Go down at D (2 threads to the right of A). Come up at A again and go down at D to make a stitch across the top. Now count 3 threads down from D and come up at E, repeating the first stitch exactly. This should break the "boring background" syndrome!

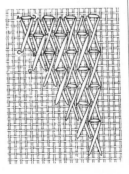

Turkey Work

I may be new to needlework, but I certainly thought someone was pulling my leg when she talked about her "Turkey work." I was embarrassed to ask her, but not you.

Think of the country and its magnificent rugs, not Thanksgiving and drumsticks! Some clever soul in the sixteenth century found a way to duplicate the luxurious, tufted effect of a Turkish carpet — in an embroidery stitch. The velvety, "sit-up" quality of the stitch makes it perfect for all sorts of fuzzy animals, insects and flower centers.

You can see from the diagram that it's actually a series of back stitches. You make a stitch, leave a loop, then let the wool lie in front. You make another stitch right back into the first and pull tight. Now with the wool at the back again, you make your loop, then go across in front, do another back stitch and pull tightly. That little back stitch in the front locks your loops in place. You can cut the loops or leave them whole. Remember to keep your stitches very tiny; otherwise, when you snip the loops, you'll have bare patches where you made too big a space between stitches.

When you stitch rows of Turkey work, complete the whole section before snipping, or all those tufts will get in your way. The best way to do the trimming is to just cut right over the top of your shape, snipping several pieces at a time. And won't you be surprised to see how much darker your wool seems! That's because the "tufts" absorb light. I always encourage beginners to practice with a gigantic piece of wool and a huge dagger of a needle, because this magnified way of stitching will show how the stitch works. I think you'll discover, when you've completed a design, that no other embroidery stitch has quite the personality of Turkey work.

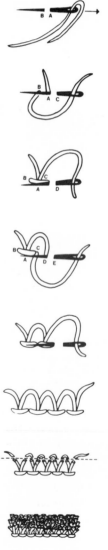

Use of Stitches

I've made a crewel sampler, but I still get stumped when it comes to working out designs. Just what stitches go where?

Your problem is one that people have so often that I've drawn up a little (well, not so little!) list of some suggestions on what stitches seem to look best on what kind of design.

For centers and circles: buttonhole, padded satin stitch, bullion knots worked side by side across the circle, French knots, Turkey work.

For leaves: close herringbone, laid work, long and short, stem stitch worked closely.

For petals: the same as for leaves, and also trellis and weaving.

For fruits and vegetables: split, long and short, brick, burden, French knots, spider's web, chain, coral, fishbone.

For birds: all kinds of laid work, buttonhole, bullions, Turkey work (for chicks).

For animals: stem, chain, split, Turkey work, satin, split, French knots.

For faces: split, stem, satin, French knot (for eyes), back stitch.

For trees: French knots on stalks, close herringbone, laid work, raised seeding.

For the sky: long and short, long lines of split stitch (open), cloud filling, laid work, running stitches, straight stitches, seeding.

For the sea: lines of split and stem, burden, chevron filling, couching, French knots, straight stitches.

For houses: brick stitch, burden, laid work, satin, squared fillings, couching, buttonhole, raised stem and back stitch.

Well, I suppose I could go on, but since there are no hard-and-fast rules about which stitch where, I think I'll let you experiment for yourself. Finding the perfect stitch for a particular shape is part of the fascination, and the art, of expert needlework.

Velvet

I once thought that doing gold work on linen was the ultimate challenge. Now that I've conquered that, I'd like to try gold on velvet. But how do I get my design onto the velvet?

You've chosen the most difficult, but one of the most satisfying, fabrics to work with. When you transfer to velvet, the pile often shifts and the design is placed inaccurately. Because the pile flattens out irregularly when you stitch, you're limited to couching, padded satin and laid and other stitches that lie smoothly on the pile. There is, however, a foolproof way to transfer: overlay the velvet with fine net, tulle or organdy with the design already traced on it. Embroider through both layers, then cut away the net closely all around. Although this method comes from the fourteenth century, there's a great twentieth-century substitute for net called Stitch Witchery or Wonderunder. These are trade names for the Pellon which tears away easily around the design — no cutting at all!

How do I remove the creases from my (imitation) velvet crazy quilt pillow top?

Prop your iron on its back in the sitting position and throw a wet cloth over it. Clouds of steam will come billowing out. (I hope you haven't just returned from the beauty parlor!) Stretch your velvet out taut about an inch from the steam you've created. If it's a very definite crease, smooth the crease back and forth just above the point of the iron for a few seconds. Another good solution is to hang your fabric in the bathroom while you run hot water from your shower. I find both methods more satisfactory than actual pressing with a regular steam iron — all that weight on your velvet won't let the pile stand up.

Wearing Your Stitches

I went to a rock concert recently (my first!) and it seemed that every pair of bluejeans had been embroidered with loving care. Can you give me some hints on how to do a pair — for my grandson, not me!

You'll be making a pair for yourself, even before you finish his, I'll bet! My first suggestion is to open up the seam of the legs first. That way you can pull out the material nice and firm in your embroidery hoop — which makes for professional, even stitching. Of course, bluejean manufacturers have made life so much easier for us by making the material soft and easy to work on. I'm sure you remember the days when you had to wash a pair of jeans 10 times to get the stiffness out.

Well, but what about your design? Anything you can do on ordinary embroidery you could translate onto jeans. Cross stitch looks great and is simple to do — all those seams around pockets, collars and cuffs really force you to keep your stitches absolutely straight. You might try using "Ombre" embroidery thread, which is streaked with different intensities of one color, to run a rainbow in Roumanian stitch across a pocket. And, unless he already has it, why not give your grandson the "frayed look." Just take pieces of cut-out denim (patches, actually) and attach them to your fabric. If you stitch slightly inside the patch border, the frayed stitches will stick out and give a "hobo" effect. And what would better suggest the "anything goes" attitude than to add a few glittering beads, held down securely with the couching stitch. Once you start on jeans, I'm sure you'll want to try out every stitch and every technique you know on them! And after jeans, there are T-shirts, the most personal kind of "billboard" advertising today. Your needle will be in steady demand with the young set.

Wearing Your Stitches

I'm not tired of my canvas beach tote bag, but everyone else is! How can I give it a new look and save my reputation?

Here's something I tried with great success on my television program: a band of honeycomb stitch on plastic canvas, making a stiff border for the base of your canvas bag. Cut the plastic canvas to size. Using 2 threads of dark Persian yarn, work a row of herringbone stitch. Count 5 threads down and 6 over to make the first diagonal. Come up 1 thread to the left, level with the last stitch, and repeat, slanting at the opposite angle. Continue along the line. Repeat the first row, working with a shade lighter beside it, 1 thread away. Continue, repeating so that the final band has 1 row of dark, 2 of medium, 1 of medium light and 2 of the lightest color. Repeat in the opposite direction below, working directly under the first dark row, coming up in the same holes as this row. Continue, completing the row.

Now with contrasting wool or cotton floss, fill in the open space left between the stitches with vertical satin stitch. To make the stitches fill the area well, it is sometimes necessary to pull back the stitching gently with your needle. You notice from the directions that the stitch is worked horizontally on the canvas. But to get the "honeycomb" effect, you just turn the canvas vertically. Naturally, in measuring your canvas and in counting out the number of finished "combs" you'll need, you have to take this into consideration. And you'll be singing the praises of plastic canvas as you work: no pulling out of shape, no frayed edges, and so easy to stitch to your old favorite tote! And just think of the time you will save by not having to block the finished piece. If you want to line the border, just stitch the fabric to the plastic canvas before you attach the whole piece to your tote.

I promised a friend I'd knit a sweater for her birthday —but the time has come and I must rush out and buy one instead. Could I add some personal touch to it?

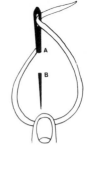

Thank heaven for the "lazy daisy" stitch when we're in a hurry! Buy one of those knubby knits (those Irish fisherman's sweaters are just right), then you can stitch all kinds of flowers on the ready-made background of the knitting. Use a good rug wool that is heavy enough for the flowers to sit up nice and plump. You'll find the lazy daisy one of the most versatile and simple of stitches. And it's so easy to create a design as you stitch; you don't have to put any pattern on your sweater first. Don't pull your stitches too tight, since the last thing you want are puckered daisies! Of course, you can tell by the diagram that the lazy daisy is really a detached chain stitch. You make a single chain stitch and anchor it down with a small stitch, as at the end of a row of chain.

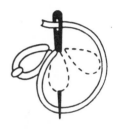

I can't throw them out but I must make my daughter's jeans fit for appearing in public. How can I patch her matchless jeans?

This is a rescue operation I've done dozens of times. Try some bluejean appliqués in those strategic places, using those great time-savers put out under the brand names Stitch Witchery or Wonderunder. These actually let you iron shapes onto fabric without sewing. Put the Stitch Witchery on top of some plastic from a dry cleaner's bag, then put your fabric on top. Give the fabric a squirt of water with a plant sprayer and put a warm iron over the 3 layers for just the count of 5 — no longer. Your fabric and Stitch Witchery are basted together! Now cut out your shape and iron it onto the jeans. You can take a light stitch around the edges as a final step, making doubly sure it can stand many washings!

Weaving Stitch

After my course in weaving, I began to think about adapting the weaving technique to needlepoint. Do you have some hints?

No problem at all! Because weaving stitches are as old as fabric itself, you can choose from a great variety of techniques and stitches. A block of weaving, like sock darning, can be done entirely on the surface. Or horizontal rows of running stitches can be woven through existing fabric. Let me show you the "weaving stitch" that is most effective done with 2 or 3 threads in the needle. When the weaving is completed evenly, the result is a series of perfect squares in contrasting colors. Follow the diagram: come up at A, down at B, up at C, down at D, etc., laying threads side by side (the width of 1 thread apart). Now change to a blunt tapestry needle. Using a contrasting color, come up at M. Weave under and over the threads, starting through the center (the widest part). Go down through the material at N. Now come up through the material at O, and weave through the threads; go down at P, up at Q, continuing to Z, pushing threads together so that even squares of each color are obtained. Finally, go back to the center and finish the lower part.

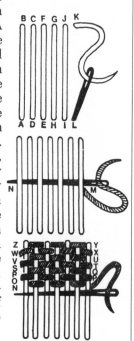

I've heard of a kind of drawn-thread work called "needle weaving." What is this?

Needle weaving is the technique (and the art) of drawing out threads from a background material, such as linen, leaving a warp, which is then woven with the needle into new patterns to make bands and borders. By all means, try it, remembering that all weaving should be done with a blunt needle to avoid any damage to the threads that have been left in to make the warp.

White Embroidery

In making a final inventory of my great-grandmother's things, I discovered rows and rows of linens, all with the most perfectly done white on white embroidery. She's not here to tell me how she did it —and I know she never owned a sewing machine.

You've discovered one of the "forgotten" needlework arts — white embroidery. And your great-grandmother didn't need a sewing machine, since machines were originally invented to imitate the delicate fineness of her handwork. Of course, white work is always done with white thread on a white background, but within these limitations all kinds of exciting and different designs are possible. You'll soon see that every stitch has a unique texture of its own — whether it be light and airy cut work (a shadow effect with sheet fabric and heavy thread), open-hole work done by pulling tightly on the thread or simple padded stitching. Your great-grandmother would be thrilled if you'd carry on her art.

Why not start by getting a bed sheet with its scalloped turnback already machine-buttonholed. (Let the machine do all the boring, repetitious parts.) Then you can make it splendid with your own cut-work eyelet embroidery. In the first step of the diagram you see the line of running stitches going all around the outline. Use a thread long enough to complete working the full circle. Leaving the thread hanging, cut 4 slits in the material from the center, out to the running stitch, as shown in the diagram. Fold back these 4 flaps, one at a time, and closely sew over and over all around the edge, working right over the running stitch. At the end, the over-sewing stitches should make a smooth banding around the edge. Cut off the frayed turnbacks neatly around the stitches on the wrong side of the sheet.

White Embroidery

I'd like to try to duplicate the raised, surface stitching that is on a very old (more than 100 years, I'm told) bedspread that came from Ireland. It's a very bold stitch done with heavy white cotton. What stitch is it?

It might be the Mountmellick stitch, since that's named for a town in Ireland where it originated. Work the stitch vertically. Begin by making a slanting stitch, but in the second step, do not go through the material. Now, take a vertical stitch, going into the same holes from A to C, and, looping the thread under the needle, draw through to complete 1 stitch. Repeat the first step, taking another stitch under the first, exactly like B to C. When you repeat the third step, go down inside the previous stitch, just like a chain. Don't restrict yourself to white on white — it looks beautiful in any color.

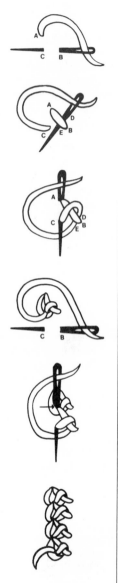

I became fascinated by white embroidery, but when I looked it up in the library, I got so confused! There are so many different styles and names —Hardanger, Hedebo, Richelieu, Reticella, Battenberg — shall I just give up?

Not before you hear this good news — all white work can be divided into just 2 types, coarse and fine. Coarse white can be worked on any opaque fabric which shows clear individual threads, from burlap weaves to the finest linen. You count the mesh to make geometric surface textures, draw out threads to form lacy patterns and borders or cut the material to make open-work holes. Fine white is done when the linen is too sheer to draw threads, so the effect is made either by letting in net, working shadow stitch on the reverse side, or by drawing the fine threads together to give an effect of open holes.

Xeroxing Designs

I've followed your instructions for transferring a design onto canvas using the graph method, and that worked perfectly fine. But now I want to do something different — reproduce a favorite color photograph of my prize rose bush in full bloom. The color variations are so subtle, I wonder how I can be sure to re-create them accurately?

You may be just the person who's been waiting for what must be one of the newest developments in transferring designs — color Xeroxing. You can have your photograph enlarged and transferred in color to canvas. It's a heat process that covers the canvas with a thin film of paint, in the colors of the original. You must work the canvas in an embroidery frame, because you'll have to "stab" your needle through the stiff paint, so you'll need your canvas stiff and taut. Of course, when you begin to match your yarn to the printed colors on the canvas, you should take advantage of the endless possibilities of color.

I've never been an advocate of exact reproduction when it comes to needlework. Like a painting, I think a needlework tapestry (which is what your rose garden will actually be!) should be translated or re-created, rather than slavishly imitated. Simply put, a photograph is a photograph, but a tapestry is another medium of expression altogether. Even though this new method of color reproduction is one of the latest things on the market, it has aroused much interest, if the inquiries I have received are any indication. I'm sure you will want to go on, using the photograph not just as a pattern to be followed, but rather as a prompter for your own imagination. Think of the additional vitality and movement you could give almost any design with just a few dashes of color and here and there a spontaneous line or two.

Yarn

I'm always left with armfuls of extra yarn at the end of my crewel projects. Is there any way of knowing from the start just how much I'll really need?

Unless you know in advance what kinds of stitches (and in what color) you'll be using, it's pretty difficult to be exact. There is a mathematical way, if you have the skill. Work a 1-inch square on your canvas and note the amount of yarn used. Figure the number of square inches to be covered by each color of your design, then multiply by the amount used to work the 1-inch square. This will give you the approximate yardage for each color and, we hope, mere handfuls left over!

I'm working — simultaneously — a crewel and a needlepoint project. But the manufacturer has run out of the original dye lot I used for some colors and the new ones are off!

You have one problem, but two solutions, so take heart! The textured stitches of crewel embroidery don't really demand an absolute match, so the new dye lot is safe. With needlepoint, and those large flat areas of colors, the solution is different. If you do have any of the old wool left, use it to fill in the area closest to the design. The slightly different tone of the new wool won't show up if it's farther from the design. But why not capitalize on the problem by creating a "striated background"? Different threads of varying shades of the same color are worked in random stripes so that there is in fact no one, solid background. Besides making for fewer gray hairs, it produces a very effective result, with the design silhouetted against the soft, blended background. Many prized antique pieces were done this way.

I'm a beginning crewel embroiderer, and I'm a bit hazy about the kind of yarn to buy and how many strands to use when I stitch.

There's no harm in repeating the basics! Real crewel wool is two-ply, firm and not too "stretchy." It is sold in small hanks in a good variety of colors. There really are no rules about whether you should use 1, 2 or more threads. One of the advantages of having a fine wool to begin with is that you can vary the number of threads according to the effect you want. Experience and practice will help you decide, and you'll find that varying the thickness in one piece of work helps to create an intriguing texture, as does combining silk or mercerized cotton with the wool in parts of the design.

I never know how many threads to use when I start a new piece of needlepoint. Are there any rules to follow?

Although the basic rules are 1 thread of Persian wool for 18 and 20 mesh, 2 threads for 14 and 12, 2 or 3 for 10, 6 (or 1 of rug wool) for 7, etc. — all canvases vary slightly, so you'll really find out only by trying a small block of stitches out on an edge of your canvas. It's safer to use fewer threads, because you can always go over with more threads if needed.

On the other hand, if you use too many threads, the stitches will be thick and uneven, the canvas threads will pack tightly together, and you'll hardly be able to force the needle between them. And if that's not enough, you probably have to cut out all your stitches and begin again! If you do reach that stage, remember to cut out your stitches from the back, because on the reverse there are longer stitches and hence more wool to get hold of. Cut the stitches on the back, then rub your scissors over the front to loosen them up, then pull out what you can — weeping silently!

Zigzag Stitching

Although I love my various needlework and quilting projects, I am addicted to my sewing machine — especially when I get it to do a decorative zigzag stitch. My question is: would it be considered an amateur's shortcut to machine stitch appliqué pieces to the background material of my table mats?

There's nothing amateurish about something expertly done. So while resorting to your sewing machine might shock some of the purists among us, we've learned that there's nothing "illegitimate" when it comes to doing needlework these days.

The best way to coordinate your machine work with your hand work is to use the zigzag stitching as a decorative edging on your appliqué table mats. If you work the machine stitch very closely, the zigzag will actually turn into a broad border — then, without even expecting it, you have the effect of a satin stitch! What could be more decorative and at the same time as practical? Another decided advantage of this method is that you won't have to take turnbacks; your raw edges will be smoothly covered, and your table mats will be strong enough to throw into the machine for the frequent washings they usually get.

You might also want to experiment with another way of using your machine in conjunction with your hand-wrought stitches. Why not run an edge of your machine zigzag stitches, and then parallel this row with a much more authentic and more textured row of an embroidery stitch in the same pattern? There are any number of variations on the herringbone stitch (closed, interlaced, threaded and tied) that will put your machine to shame!

I suppose the whole idea is just daring to break the rules — and that's the secret and much of the fun of *needleplay!*

THE VARIETY OF NEEDLEWORK

Throughout the pages of this book, you
have been shown diagrams of scores of
individual stitches. Now I would like you
to see, in the following section, how the
various needlework stitches and techniques
look when worked as completed designs.
Crewel, needlepoint, crewelpoint, black
and white work, stump work, bargello and
shisha are illustrated, with examples taken
from museum pieces as well as from
contemporary projects.

All the needlework illustrated on these
pages was designed and worked by the
author, except for the Elizabethan mitten
on page 126 (courtesy Victoria and Albert
Museum) and the tree of life on page 115,
which was designed by Wilanna Bristow.

Crewel embroidery designed as a sampler, with 26 different stitches.

Contemporary tree of life design with a variety of crewel stitches;
chevron stitch in the tree bark.

Elizabethan lady in black and gold work; compare with the same design in three-dimensional stump work, page 123.

Darning on net. A frame or hoop is useful for working stitches.

Fine white work on lawn, illustrating trailing and open filling.

Shadow work on organdie.

Combined white work stitches on organdie.

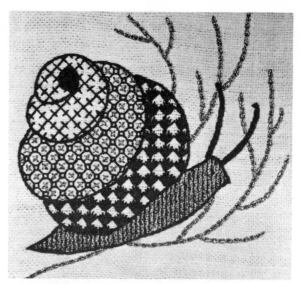

Black work snail enriched with gold thread.

Black work pattern on even-weave linen.

Man's vest with patterns in black silk, cotton and gold on fine linen.

Bargello patterns. Upper left is a kaleidoscope design with bargello worked on four sides of a square.

Stump work. The Elizabethan lady's skirt is worked on No. 18
needlepoint canvas, then applied to the background.

Needlepoint designs created with simple tent stitch worked in stripes.

Textured canvas: crewelpoint (crewel and needlepoint stitches) combined with tent stitch in one design.

Crewelpoint, with horse's mane in bullion knot worked on top.

Gold butterfly in couching stitches; mille fleur pattern in wings.

Elizabethan mitten, silk and gold embroidery, satin with velvet.

Shisha work, or Indian mirror embroidery.

Index of Stitches